About Island Press

Since 1984, the nonprofit Island Press has been stimulating, shaping, and communicating the ideas that are essential for solving environmental problems worldwide. With more than 800 titles in print and some 40 new releases each year, we are the nation's leading publisher on environmental issues. We identify innovative thinkers and emerging trends in the environmental field. We work with world-renowned experts and authors to develop cross-disciplinary solutions to environmental challenges.

Island Press designs and implements coordinated book publication campaigns in order to communicate our critical messages in print, in person, and online using the latest technologies, programs, and the media. Our goal: to reach targeted audiences—scientists, policymakers, environmental advocates, the media, and concerned citizens—who can and will take action to protect the plants and animals that enrich our world, the ecosystems we need to survive, the water we drink, and the air we breathe.

Island Press gratefully acknowledges the support of its work by the Agua Fund, Inc., The Margaret A. Cargill Foundation, Betsy and Jesse Fink Foundation, The William and Flora Hewlett Foundation, The Kresge Foundation, The Forrest and Frances Lattner Foundation, The Andrew W. Mellon Foundation, The Curtis and Edith Munson Foundation, The Overbrook Foundation, The David and Lucile Packard Foundation, The Summit Foundation, Trust for Architectural Easements, The Winslow Foundation, and other generous donors.

Common Ground on Hostile Turf

COMMON GROUND ON HOSTILE TURF

Stories from an Environmental Mediator

Lucy Moore

ISLANDPRESS
Washington | Covelo | London

Library of Congress Cataloging-in-Publication Data

Moore, Lucy, 1944–

Common ground on hostile turf : stories from an environmental mediator / Lucy Moore.

pages cm.

Summary: "As an environmental mediator, Lucy Moore has spent the past quarter century resolving conflicts that appeared utterly intractable. Here, she shares the ten most compelling stories of her career"— Provided by publisher.

ISBN 978-1-61091-410-9 (hardback) — ISBN 1-61091-410-4 (cloth)— ISBN 978-1-61091-411-6 (paper) 1. Environmental policy. 2. Environmental protection. 3. Environmental mediation. 4. Conflict management. I. Title.

GE170.M635 2013

333.7—dc23

2013005860

Printed on recycled, acid-free paper

Text design by Joyce C. Weston

Manufactured in the United States of America

10 9 8 7 6 5 4 3 2 1

Keywords: Island Press, mediation, conflict resolution, facilitation, public involvement, stakeholder, natural resources, natural resource conflicts, multiparty multi-issue conflict, consensus building, environmental conflict resolution, environmental mediation, public policy, decision making, consensus decision making, public policy disputes, public policy mediation, cross-cultural communication, tribal issues, tribal consultation, Native American governments, Navajo, Pojoaque Pueblo, Ganados del Valle woolgrowers cooperative, Hispanic communities, Land Grants (New Mexico), uranium, Superfund site, U.S. Department of the Interior, U.S. Environmental Protection Agency, U.S. Bureau of Indian Affairs, U.S. Army Corps of Engineers, environmental resource, toxic waste siting, education, dam management

For Roberto Gallegos

whose loving support helped make this book a reality

Contents

Preface *xi*

Acknowledgments *xiii*

Chapter 1. Introduction 1

Chapter 2. Encountering Hostile Turf 9

Chapter 3. The Power of Story 23

Chapter 4. Sheep in the Wilderness 33

Chapter 5. Finding Common Ground 69

Chapter 6. The Army Corps Takes Orders 87

Chapter 7. A Rugged Road 103

Chapter 8. So Close to Consensus 117

Chapter 9. When the Past Won't Go Away 131

Chapter 10. When Cookies Aren't Enough 147

Chapter 11. Tribes Take the Lead 161

Chapter 12. Conclusion 179

About the Author *193*

Index *195*

Preface

After painting a very grim picture of a future world impacted by climate change, author and environmentalist Bill McKibben was asked where he would move in order to have the best chance of surviving. Where on the planet, asked the questioner, would one's chances be the best? He smiled. Although people who ask that question are usually thinking in terms of geography—where can I go to escape the rising oceans, the killer drought, the devastating floods?—he said that the answer, in his opinion, was not a geographic one. "I would look for a place to go," he said, "where there is a community that can make decisions together. That is the kind of place where survival is possible."

His remarks at the Quivira Coalition's 2011 conference in Albuquerque were exciting for me because I have tried for decades to create those "communities" where decisions are made collectively, where decisions include and respect the full diversity of interests. My communities are not usually "communities of place" but rather "communities of interest," where those who have come together share a common problem, strive for a common goal, or seek to resolve a conflict.

As an environmental and public policy mediator for the past twenty-five years, I have been in the middle of dozens of highly controversial regional and national conflicts. Each, of course, is different. There are those that make the drive or the flight home a joyful time for happy reflection. There are those that wake me up at night, and in that distorted time when all things frightening rush in, I despair over my community, my country, the world.

Both the human and the natural worlds are under enormous stress. My cases are illustrations of our need to make critical choices as conflicting demands from a growing and mobile population increase. We need to extract natural resources to have the quality of life we want. We want to live with open space and recreational opportunities in our backyards. We need ranchers and farmers to feed us. We want to preserve species while we are making their survival unlikely. We want our children educated, yet other priorities seem to come first. We want to be respected, but we have a hard time respecting others. Without a way to resolve these conflicts in an equitable and sustainable way, the battles will continue and the hostility among interests will escalate.

The circuitous path to a collective answer is defined by personalities, culture, power, and how we feel about one another. One of the mediator's most important contributions toward resolving any dispute is providing the space—physical and emotional—where those in conflict can tell their stories to each other. In that spirit, I am offering my stories from the trenches of conflict resolution, in hopes that they will further McKibben's conversation about how we can grow and support those communities that make decisions together.

I will start by suggesting that the first step is basic human interaction in which everyone, mediator included, is able to be honest, vulnerable, open, and respectful. Once this happens, the logjam of warring studies and legal threats may break loose. The result can be a resolution that not only is equitable and sustainable but also shows that trust and respect among adversaries are possible. This is a vision that I hold dear, as a balance to the deep and real fears for the future.

Acknowledgments

I owe an enormous debt to Barbara Dean, my editor at Island Press. She encouraged and guided me with such a skillful, gentle hand, always reminding me that this was my book and that I was at the helm. The truth is I never would have made it to port without her as my first mate. Thanks to Barbara, Meghan Bartels, Pat Harris, Erin Johnson, Julie Marshall, Sharis Simonian, and others at Island Press, the experience was a complete pleasure. I am also very grateful to Beth Hadas, friend, editor, and all-around smart person, who was such a loyal and helpful companion throughout the process.

Bill deBuys, James McGrath Morris, and Elise Turner read early chapters and spurred me on with good guidance and general cheerleading. And a special thanks to Nancy Hunter Warren, to whom I read the entire manuscript aloud. Her exclamations of "Hold on!" and "I don't follow that" were invaluable to me as I made the book ready for the general reader.

I am grateful to Joanna Hurley, Irene Webb, and Liz Trupin-Pulli, who helped me make the leap from manuscript to publisher. Thanks to Antonio Manzanares and Maria Varela for digging into their memories to help enrich "Sheep in the Wilderness" and to Matt Magoffin, Bill McDonald, and Bill Miller for help with "A Rugged Road."

I have shared my work life with wonderful colleagues: at Western Network, John Folk-Williams, Eileen Frueh, Carl Moore, Richard Pacheco, and Rosemary Romero; and in private practice, Dexter Albert, Roberto Chené, Seth Cohen, Saman Hussain, Ed Moreno, and Jon Townsend. Each has brought life, warmth, and wisdom to the projects we've done together.

Thank you to friends and wise advisors Sandy Blakeslee, Marion Cox, Sally Denton, Mary Davis Hamlin, David Lujan, Marla Painter, and Luis Torres; to the Meeting Ground folks who taught me so much, Roberto

Chené, Mary Ann Lundy, Peter Pino, Roberta Rael, Nadine Tafoya, and Nahum Ward-Lev; and to my fellow Thursday morning seekers.

My training as a mediator began years before I mediated my first case, when fresh out of college I worked for Robert Coles, author and child psychiatrist. He taught me how to listen, deeply and with an open heart, to the voices of people under stress, a skill I have treasured all my life. I am also very grateful to my mentors Howard Bellman, Gary Friedman, and Ben Moya, extraordinary mediators who gave me the courage to step into the middle of conflict. But the real lessons that have shaped me as a mediator came from all the characters in these stories, who taught, tested, and inspired me.

Finally, to dear friends Chris Nunn Garcia, David Henderson, and Arón Rael, who were heroes for me and have passed on, I send my thanks and affection.

CHAPTER ONE

Introduction

Jacob Viarrial, governor of the Pueblo of Pojoaque, sat at a folding table next to Richard Lucero, the mayor of Española, New Mexico. They were at the front of a linoleum-floored all-purpose meeting room at the pueblo that served as council chambers, senior activities center, and, on this particular day, a place to talk with neighbors about groundwater contamination. The walls were covered with photos of the governor's parents and grandparents, his ten siblings, and others from earlier days at the pueblo.

When the chairs were filled and the time seemed right, the governor leaned over to consult with the mayor and then stood up and moved behind a simple wooden podium. He was of average height and above average weight, with dark, curly hair and a face that could have belonged to a prizefighter. His features reflected his heritage, Hispanic and Pueblo, but they seemed to have been beaten into place, with a kind of lumpy result. His forehead and prominent nose were beaded with sweat—as they were in any weather, I would later learn—giving the impression that he was really hot, really nervous, or seriously ill.

He welcomed everyone and told a joke, clearly to warm himself up. I could tell he was nervous but also that he was a powerful leader, able to use that nervousness to win over an audience. Everyone laughed at the joke—about three Indians in a boat, patterned after three lawyers in a boat, three religious leaders in a boat, and so on—and then the governor began to explain how this meeting came to be.

He introduced Mayor Lucero and said that the two of them had met recently in Española at a restaurant and had talked about the groundwater quality crisis they, as neighbors, shared. The state had sampled several wells in the area and found high levels of nitrates, probably coming from septic tanks sited too close to wells. The population in the valley was exploding and, with it, the number of wells and septic tanks. Something had to be done, he said, but—and here he hesitated and took a drink of water from his coffee mug—with all the hostility between the pueblo and its neighbors, it was going to be tough.

He was referring to the monster water rights adjudication known as *Aamodt*, named after the first person in an alphabetized list of thousands of defendants, all water users living in the basins formed by three small tributaries to the Rio Grande. Filed by the State of New Mexico in 1966 for the purpose of clarifying—"perfecting" is the legal term—the water rights in the water-short region just north of Santa Fe, the *Aamodt* suit has become famous as the longest-living federal litigation. Back in 1987, when the governor called this meeting of his neighbors, it was twenty-one years old and had already wreaked havoc on relationships in the valleys.

Because in New Mexico the state engineer begins the adjudication process by *suing* every water user in the basin, what is supposed to be a straightforward administration of water rights—deciding who has the right to how much water—becomes a legal battle between the state and each water user and, inevitably, among all the water users. The adjudication process is incredibly complicated as the state tries to balance the claims of individuals, irrigation districts, municipalities, and industries with Indian rights and federal interests. The existence of an endangered species, the needs of a federal agency, the unpredictability of rain and snowfall, and the relationship between surface water and groundwater can add more layers of complexity and more years to the life span of the adjudication. Users are pitted against one another in a battle over every drop. There is serious social and economic fallout from the uncertainty of future water supplies, the fierce competition for scarce water, and the litigious forum for decision making.

This was not always the system in northern New Mexico. Neighbors for centuries, Pueblo and Hispanic communities traditionally shared the scarce resource proportionately. In a dry year, those with land farther upstream—usually the Pueblos—would take less water so that their neighbors below weren't left dry. But since statehood in 1912, New Mexico has lived by the prior appropriation doctrine, which grants a full water right to whatever entity first put the water to use, the one with the earliest priority date. Those who put water to use at a later date are junior rights holders and must allow the senior rights holders to take their full portion of water first before taking theirs.

As the earliest documented users of water in the basin, the pueblos in the Pojoaque and Española Valleys sit in a very favorable position. Their Hispanic neighbors come in second, with dates from the 1700s and 1800s, and Anglo newcomers are usually last in line. Legally, the four Indian pueblos in the valley could end up with the right to take all the water they needed before any other needs were satisfied. Non-Indian residents in the valley panicked at this prospect, and the pueblos became the target of fear and animosity. Demonstrators carried empty buckets and "We Need Water, Too" signs in front of the courthouse in Santa Fe. Children waiting for a school bus reportedly threw rocks at Pueblo kids because they were "taking our water." On that July morning in 1987 when the governor invited his neighbors—Anglo, Hispanic, and Pueblo—to the council chamber, the situation created by the *Aamodt* adjudication was in crisis.

"I want to make a rule right now," he said, "and the rule is that in this room, as long as we're meeting here at the pueblo, no one will say the word that starts with 'A.' You all know the word I mean, and I'm not going to say it, and neither is anyone else. Anyone says the 'A' word, they're out of here," and he flung a stubby finger at the door. There was silence. Everyone knew the governor was right. If anything constructive were to happen, the lawsuit that had shaped their lives for over two decades would have to be off the table.

"And one more thing," he said, pulling a big red kerchief out of his pocket and mopping his forehead and nose. "I told the mayor that we should meet here at Pojoaque because this is Indian land, and I can keep the press out! The mayor doesn't have that ability, but I do, and that is another rule. There will be no press at these meetings. They've done too much to drive us apart, and we don't need that here." This brought applause. Now the governor was at ease, and his passion poured out.

He invited audience members to speak, and several did, relating anecdotes about the water contamination and expressing hope that this kind of cooperation might work. Mayor Lucero spoke on behalf of the town of Española, pledging to work as neighbors and partners to produce safe drinking water for all valley residents. "This contamination knows no boundaries," he pointed out. "It will pollute all our wells, Indian and non-Indian. This is not an issue to fight over; it's an issue to fight together." The meeting ended with thanks from Lucero and Viarrial to those in attendance.

The governor said that everyone was welcome to stay for lunch, compliments of the pueblo, and as if by magic four women appeared, all relatives of the governor, with big aluminum pans of enchiladas, Crock-Pots full of red chile stew, bread, Jell-O salad, and cake. Most people stayed; the smell of the food and the chatter of neighbors were too enticing.

The Española and Pojoaque Valleys Water and Wastewater Steering Committee, born that day, became a force for progress and good health in the valleys for several years. It had no bylaws or mission statement; the members were whoever showed up that day. The one certainty was the lunch, always worth the trip. Grants were written, projects were funded, there were water fairs and school poster contests, and a brand-new sewage facility was built to safely treat what was pumped from the septic tanks. Governor Viarrial guided the group, sometimes with more cheer than at other times, sometimes frustrated by what he had read in the paper that morning, but never giving up. He and I developed a close relationship as I took on the role of note taker and, eventually, facilitator for the meetings.

He applied that same perseverance and courage to promoting his pueblo. He was determined to make his community self-supporting, but with such a small population (fewer than 500), any federal aid from the Bureau of Indian Affairs was meaningless. "Our criminal justice division doesn't get enough money," he said to me in one of our early conversations, "to buy one police car. It's barely enough to buy the tires!" He had put his pueblo on the map with a destination resort, golf courses and casinos, a cultural center and museum offering classes in art and culture, and a state-of-the-art tribal government complex. In the process, however, he had engendered a new wave of controversy. He was impetuous, outspoken, often outrageous in his advocacy for his people, with little concern for the consequences. In a protest over state taxation, he ordered tribal police to close the highway that ran through the pueblo linking Santa Fe, Los Alamos, and Taos. And of course he was criticized for using precious groundwater on his golf courses. His answer was simple: mainstream society has been building golf courses and making money for a long time; now it's our turn. But throughout this stormy career, he continued to try to build bridges with neighbors and never lost his sense of humor and his willingness to take risks. And he always made sure to feed people. He died in 2004 at the age of fifty-eight. The *Aamodt* suit, finally settled in 2010, outlived him.

For me, that first meeting with Governor Viarrial was thrilling. I saw someone, a significant player in a serious conflict, with the courage to stand up in front of his enemies and suggest that there was a better way to coexist. He asked them to set aside the hostility, and said that he would do the same, in order to address a shared environmental crisis. He led them to a common ground where they could be neighbors in the true sense of the word. I saw the power that lies in an individual willing to be vulnerable in front of the enemy in the interest of solving a problem together. I was hooked.

Since that early experience twenty-five years ago, I have mediated dozens of highly controversial regional and national conflicts concerning the allocation, use, and management of natural resources and the development of public policy. I have seen the power of a personality, such as Jake Viarrial's, make or break a process. I have marveled at how cultural differences of all kinds—from corporate to ethnic—can keep a good solution from moving forward. I have discovered the value of anecdotal knowledge in a sea of technical data. I have learned how to deal with historical trauma when it rises to the surface and threatens to sink a resolution. I have learned that for the mediator, as well as those at the table, it is critical to understand and honor the human side of conflict.

This book offers a fresh look at conflict resolution through my eyes as a mediator. It is a collection of stories that illustrate some of the most thorny challenges I have faced while struggling in the trenches of environmental and public policy mediation. I hope that my experiences will be relevant to a broad audience—professional and lay—and that the reader will find them instructive, entertaining, and above all thought provoking. For my fellow mediators, this will be a chance to squirm, groan, and laugh as you see me in predicaments you know all too well. For the classroom, the book provides real examples of the polarization that undergraduate and graduate students will encounter in their chosen field—environmental studies, public policy, resource management, and conflict resolution, to name a few. And, depending on the role they choose, they will come away with some insights to help warring parties find that common ground. Finally, the general reader will find lively stories with memorable moments, as well as a basic education about some of the major resource issues in the West today. In this age of increasing conflict with higher and higher stakes, we all need a heightened awareness and some practical strategies for dealing with what lies ahead.

I am addicted to stories, as you can already see. The next ten chapters describe cases that for me are memorable. Selecting the stories among dozens that I could have told was torture, like choosing among one's children. Those included here are in chronological order and illustrate a challenge, an insight, or a difficult choice that guided my development as a mediator. They also contain strong personalities, good story lines, and an element of suspense. I let the stories speak for themselves, sometimes identifying themes but generally leaving the reader to absorb whatever lesson emerges. Chapter 4, "Sheep in the Wilderness," I see as a kind of centerpiece for the book. It is longer than the others in order to tell a particularly compelling and complex story that was critical in my early years as a mediator. Chapter 12, the conclusion, pulls together the lessons and reflections in a more coherent format.

A mediator must be able to keep the confidences of the parties in the conflict. I have been careful to change names in most of the cases, retaining real names only with permission. In some of the cases there was a co-mediator for some of the time. For the sake of simplicity, I have usually not included these colleagues in the stories, but their contributions to my evolution as a mediator have been great.

I identify myself as an environmental mediator, and most of my work involves the use and management of natural resources. But, like many who work in the multiparty, multi-issue arena, I take other cases as well. Chapters 3, 9, and 11 deal with national public policy relating to tribal education and sovereignty.

I use the terms "mediator" and "facilitator" throughout the book. Generally, a mediator helps resolve a specific dispute, while a facilitator may manage a variety of processes, including public meetings, workshops, and dialogues that may have other goals, such as sharing information or drafting a work plan. For me the two functions are so closely linked that I often make no distinction. Both involve helping people communicate to move forward to a common goal.

Finally, a word about what mediation is and does. The standard definition of a mediator is a neutral person who helps those in conflict find their own solution. This is based on the assumption that those who are embroiled in the conflict know it best and therefore know where the opportunities for resolution are. Although it is sometimes very tempting, the mediator will not make a decision for the parties, no matter how stuck they get. If mediation does not produce a resolution, the parties can turn to arbitration or the courts or duke it out in the press or the next election.

But I like my colleague Peter Adler's definition of mediation best. He says that what he does is simply help people tell their stories to each other. Once the table is set, the ground rules are in place, and parties take their seats, the mediator's job, he says, is to help people express themselves honestly and to ensure that others are genuinely listening. Of course, the table conversation can be quite complex. In this book you will find conflicts involving water rights, toxic waste disposal, Indian education, ranching, reservoir management, and more, with solutions that are complicated and costly. They may involve changes in legislation or regulation, the siting of major facilities, the protection or development of significant resources. But I believe there is an important truth here and that Peter is right: it is all about the story. I invite you to read on and see for yourself.

CHAPTER TWO

Encountering Hostile Turf

I began my mediation career with Western Network, a non-profit founded by my colleague and friend John Folk-Williams in the late 1980s. John and I were committed to working in our own backyard, albeit a backyard neither of us had known for more than a few years. We saw that northern New Mexico, a region rich in tradition and culture, was under great stress and hoped we could help. There were conflicts over land and water resources, against a backdrop of cross-cultural tension and a high rate of poverty. What was needed, we concluded, was a way to bring communities, interest groups, and government agencies together to resolve some of these disputes. The communities were primarily Hispanic or Indian, the interest groups environmental or business, and the agencies state or federal. Most of our funding came from private foundations, in the East and Midwest, that shared our vision of a more cooperative and equitable way of making decisions in poor rural areas. Writing proposals was a chore, but the payoff—quite literally—was worth it, and we were happy not to have to charge our "clients" for our services.

But foundation funding had a downside that took us several years to understand. This chapter follows that painful but rewarding journey as we learned about unintended consequences, accountability, and trust.

In the winter of 1987, I saw an announcement about a meeting that intrigued me. The convener was a Hispanic community organizer and friend who said I could come as an observer. The purpose of the meeting, he said, was to organize New Mexico's small irrigators to defeat an in-stream flow bill that environmental activists planned to introduce in the next legislative session. If successful, the legislation would allow for a river to have its own water rights, protecting fish, wildlife, and the riparian areas to some extent from drought and competition from other uses. At the time, water rights could be permitted only for domestic, agricultural, municipal, and industrial uses, and streams could theoretically be dried up if water rights for those uses equaled the amount of flow in the river. This was an alarming prospect, and so environmental activists had taken the initiative to legalize in-stream flow rights in New Mexico.

The fact that New Mexico was the only western state without such legislation gave environmentalists an extra impetus. As you will see throughout this book, people are driven not just by their intellectual positions and beliefs. Their emotions, their egos, their fears play large roles as well. And in this case, some of the activists expressed embarrassment that the state was an outlier under their watch. They wanted to get this bill passed and hold their heads up high among their colleagues in the other western states. The fierce opposition from the small irrigators was mystifying and disturbing to them.

These opponents were acequia (ah-say-kia) members and their associations. An acequia is a hand-dug earthen ditch designed to carry irrigation water (and in earlier times perhaps domestic water) to the point of use. For traditional Hispanic communities, acequias serve more than a water distribution function; they are both the backbone and the heart of the community. Those living along the acequia gather in the spring to clean the ditches and repair headgates. The mayordomo (overseer) of each acequia is the de facto leader of the community, the person who resolves differences between neighbors and enforces participation in community projects. An acequia association is the governing body of the community, recognized in the state constitution with certain powers and rights. There are over 200 acequia associations in New Mexico, some with only a handful of members, some with hundreds. Economically poor, acequia members are surprisingly powerful lobbyists in the legislature; they had handed the environmentalists defeat on the in-stream flow issue in the previous session.

So why would these traditional irrigators be so opposed to in-stream flow legislation, which could result in more water in the river, a healthier riparian system, and a more robust fish population?

Grassroots acequia advocates saw this seemingly benign legislation as a grave threat to their way of life. An active water rights market was emerging as developers and water brokers searched for diminishing water sources for urban growth, golf courses, and industry. The acequia communities, being poor, were especially vulnerable to the market system. Their water rights with early priority dates (in most cases, second only to the pueblos and tribes) were especially desirable to buyers because in times of shortage those with the earliest dates could take their full share before junior users were allowed a drop. If the price for an acre-foot of water went high enough, the first to fall prey and sell would be the acequia members. The life was hard, and they were tired. Children were leaving the rural life and wanting a more urban lifestyle. Selling your water rights could get you a ticket to a comfortable retirement.

If enough members succumbed and sold out, it became impossible for the remaining members to keep the system going. There would be fewer workers to maintain the ditch and the headgates, and at some point there might not even be enough water flowing through the system to make it work. (A certain minimal amount is necessary to carry the head of the water forward.) Acequia members, like other rural folks, appreciated the need for water in the river and probably preferred to see the water flowing there rather than going to cities and developers. But at this time environmentalists were the primary enemy. The environmental movement, the acequia members believed, had unlimited funds to spend in buying up water rights, and the environmentalists would drive the price higher and higher as they bid on water to leave in the stream.

This dilemma interested us at Western Network, and we hoped there would be a role for us as mediators at some point. We could talk easily with the Anglo members of the environmental community (who were like us in so many ways), we had credibility with local pueblos, and we had some familiarity with traditional Hispanic communities. Hoping to learn more about the issue, I entered the community room at the La Farge branch of the Santa Fe Public Library in Santa Fe that winter afternoon. My friend was sitting at the head of a hollow-square arrangement of tables. Every chair at the tables was filled, and most of the folding chairs along the walls were filled, too. I slipped into an empty chair near the door, happy to be inconspicuous.

The discussion was heated, but the subject was not in-stream flow. Agitated irrigators were questioning why the meeting had been called in the first place, and I felt immediate compassion for my friend, who was taking the heat. Was convening this meeting to talk about in-stream flow some kind of scheme to undermine the authority of acequias? Somehow the organizers had been cast in a role of collaborators in the evil sense, willing to discuss in-stream flow, willing perhaps to negotiate with the environmentalists. The crowd in the room was adamant that there should be no negotiation, no discussion, period. My friend agreed in general but tried to make the point that there might be environmentalists who were interested in the unintended consequences of their legislation, who might be willing to make accommodations to the acequias' needs. Wasn't that worth exploring, he asked? The answer was a resounding no.

Then came the question that made me shrink in my seat. Was this the idea of some foundation? The angry irrigator spat out the word, as if to get the bad taste out of his mouth as quickly as possible. Did the organizers get foundation funding to hold this meeting, to try to get local land-based people to cooperate with environmentalists? A Hispanic community organizer from Mora, in northern New Mexico, turned toward me. "Are you part of this meeting? Was this your idea at Western Network?" I was surprised that the man knew who I was, not understanding yet the notorious role Western Network was playing out in the rural communities. I protested that I was just there to listen and learn, that I had had no role in organizing the meeting. My friend tried to defend me, but the irrigator went on.

"We need to be sure we can trust who's here before we talk business, make sure there are no hidden agendas in here." Flustered, I said I didn't want to cause a problem and got up to leave. The man from Mora was apparently done talking, too, and followed me into the hallway. He had his jacket and cowboy hat on, ready to go, but he stopped and put out his hand and introduced himself. I shook it, suddenly aware of how small and smooth my hand was compared with his, big and rough, capable of cleaning ditches, tilling earth, roping cattle. I soon realized that he had left when I did so that he could grill me about Western Network, our foundation affiliations, and our agenda for northern New Mexico communities.

Still flustered, I tried to give the most obvious answer I could think of: we were interested in water conflicts and hoped to play a role in helping adversaries talk about difficult issues. Unable to let go of foundations, he wanted to know who paid my salary, and when I confessed that it was part of a foundation grant, he jumped on me again. Foundations were butting into the business of traditional communities, and all in the name of helping, he said. But they—and the people they funded, like me—weren't helping. We were *entremetidos*—those who interfere where they don't belong.

The man from Mora gave me a critical lesson about working with foundations in New Mexico—a lesson that I have remembered, albeit painfully, and applied in a wide variety of cases in other parts of the country and with other cultures and groups. The angry irrigator explained to me that do-gooders like me arrive in a place that is not ours, assuming we have the answers. But our ignorance of the history, the culture, the needs of the people and the landscape makes us dangerous intruders in the eyes of locals. Like the environmentalists, we bring with us connections to money and power. We speak the same language as the foundation people; we have instant credibility with them; we probably went to the same schools. (I cringed at this one, since both John and I were Harvard graduates.) Entremetidos like us offer the foundation people the opportunity to feel good, to help these romantic, impoverished farmers in northern New Mexico, by funding us at Western Network.

"Who says we need meetings, mediation, reports?" he shouted at me. "Give us the money—without the entremetidos—and we could do a lot of good for our communities." I considered walking out on him. He had insulted me and seemed to have already convicted me of being an ignorant elitist come to exploit the natives. But if there was a shred of truth in what he said, he had every right to be angry—and I had an obligation to listen. I chose to stay. We stared at each other a long time. He must have been debating the same question. Do I walk out on this hopeless case, or is there something redeemable here?

Finally, he said, "I just want to know who you are." He was still frustrated, but his face was a little less red. "Why do you care about all this? Who are you?"

My instinct was to answer professionally, but I had already tried to explain what I did, and that had only fueled the fire. I realized he was asking a different question. He wanted to know what kind of person I was, not what I did. He needed to know if he could trust me. Did I care about what he cared about? Was I honest and trustworthy? Was I interested and willing to learn about the landscape, both physical and cultural, around me? I tested the waters. "You mean you want to know about me? My life?" He nodded, and I self-consciously told him about being raised in Seattle and going east to college, admitting that he had nailed me on that and that I did have a privileged access to some people with money. I told him I had come to the Southwest to work with Navajos, and we shared a smile over those earlier do-good efforts. And now I lived in Santa Fe with my husband and two sons.

"Now we're getting somewhere," he said, softening. He asked if we owned land, and I said yes, a half acre, and then he asked if we owned water rights. I had to pause and think about it.

"No," I said, "we're on a community water system. We don't grow anything." I was struck by the question. No one had ever asked me that before, but of course it was very relevant in this conversation. I was beginning to see things from his perspective.

"Well," he said zipping up his jacket, "I've got a long drive. Maybe we'll talk more sometime." I told him I would like that and that he knew where to find me. We both indulged in a cautious laugh. As it turned out, we saw each other only one other time, years later, at the Albuquerque airport. We greeted each other with a touch of formality. He had been following my progress, he said. I waited for the other shoe to drop, but he just smiled, shook my hand, and went to catch his plane.

I took away three important lessons from that meeting. First, land-based communities in New Mexico have a deep connection to the land, a connection that comes from generations of working that soil. The past, present, and future are grounded in that connection, and in this fast-moving mainstream culture, they must protect those resources. I heard this passion laced with desperation at the meeting and then in the hall from my tutor from Mora.

It is a truth that I have seen in many parts of the country, certainly with tribal populations and with other land-based communities as well. It was expressed eloquently by Peter Pino from the Pueblo of Zia when he addressed a crowd of national water experts in Albuquerque several years ago. He pointed out that he and his people were not going anywhere. Leaving was not an option. In contrast, he said, during the introductions of the fifty lawyers and hydrologists in the room he had heard many speak of their journey as they sought education, changed jobs, looked for more compatible places to live. "You seem to move around a lot. We don't." His point was powerful. He and his people belonged in that place, historically and culturally, and they could not survive elsewhere. Economic hard times, pollution of resources, drought—nothing could drive them away.

Second, my eyes were opened to the complexity and unintended consequences of foundation funding in a poor state. The foundations' grants are badly needed, and they can make a significant improvement in the lives of many. But their actions can also be misguided; for example, they may send money to communities by way of intermediaries that may or may not be spending those funds to address the needs the community would have identified. Foundation funding can also pit applicants against one another as they compete for scarce funds. In years since, I have seen foundations try to become more accountable to those who are the intended recipients of the help. But I believe deeply that those of us with the advantages of education and access to funders must be responsible entremetidos (if there is such a thing), ensuring that the communities we claim to be helping have a role in the project, from conception through evaluation.

Finally, I learned that day that I could not simply be a mediator if I was going to work with communities in New Mexico, or elsewhere, for that matter. To work successfully I needed to gain trust, and no one was going to automatically trust the entremetido. What mattered was who I was, in a variety of contexts. In some cases, but not all, it has been important for clients and those with whom I am working to know about my personal history—where I come from originally, what ethnic heritage I claim, where I went to school, where I live, whether I have children, and so on. Sometimes this comes out in the beginning during introductions, sometimes later as we become more comfortable with one another.

Trusting the mediator is basic to resolving conflict anywhere and with any group. Mediators know that revealing something about themselves that is personal, perhaps even that makes them vulnerable, is part of building that trust. The parties want to know they are in skilled and experienced hands, but they also want to know that this technician can deal with the unexpected, can accept and learn from criticism and be honest, open, and fair. Mediators model these qualities as the opportunity arises, sometimes dramatically, as you will see in later chapters.

And finally, trust and credibility depend on my willingness to learn about and respect the nature of the landscape around me—not just geographically but also historically, culturally, psychologically, in every way possible. This mandate is loud and clear in northern New Mexico, but all of us working in conflict resolution need to focus on the landscape wherever we are. In fact, I could extrapolate and say that this kind of "landscape familiarity" also applies to work with federal agencies. In working with the US Fish and Wildlife Service or the US Army Corps of Engineers or the US Forest Service, it has been critical that I put myself in the position of a student, learning from the bureaucrats the lay of their land.

New Mexico has been a wonderful teacher, with its unique history, rich cultural foundation, and complex relationships among those waves of immigrants that have washed over the land in the past 400 years. I offer here a bit of what I have learned about my adopted homeland, because some of the chapters that follow are set in the Southwest but also to demonstrate the kind of "absorption" the mediator needs to have in order to work effectively.

Before the arrival of the Spanish in the late sixteenth century, dozens of indigenous groups occupied what is now New Mexico, living and farming in compact villages, or pueblos, along the Rio Grande. There were different languages and cultures, and there were both alliances and conflicts over available resources.

Looking for gold and converts to Catholicism, Spanish settlers and clergy came with soldiers, moving northward along the river. Some settled next door to Pueblo people, whom they assumed needed civilizing, saving, enslaving, or all three. There are accounts of brutality, notably at the hands of Governor Juan de Oñate. In retaliation for the death of his nephew, he attacked the Pueblo of Acoma, killing men, women, and children and, as a final message, cutting off the left foot of every surviving adult male, an adult being anyone over fourteen. If there is any doubt about the impact of this incident on the psyche of New Mexico, in 1998, some 400 years later, an unknown person cut off the left foot of an equestrian statue of Oñate. Newly installed, the statue stood in front of the Oñate Monument Resource and Visitors Center, on the highway between Santa Fe and Taos, a highway that links eight Rio Grande pueblos.

In 1620, in an effort to quell conflict, Felipe II, the king of Spain, declared that each pueblo should choose a governor and other officials by popular election. To commemorate this transition to European-style government, he awarded each new governor a cane, with a silver cap inscribed with a cross, to be handed down to successive leaders. Pueblos today revere their canes as symbols of their sovereignty, along with similar canes presented to them by President Abraham Lincoln in 1864.

But the canes were not enough. Weary of their colonizers, the Pueblos staged a remarkable revolt. Popé, a leader at Taos Pueblo, the most northerly on the Rio Grande, hatched a plan that involved runners carrying knotted strings to each pueblo. Each pueblo leader was instructed to untie one knot each day, and when the knots were gone, that would be the day of the revolt. On August 10, 1680, the Pueblos took their Spanish neighbors by surprise simultaneously, before any could give a warning to the others. They killed hundreds, and the rest fled south through Santa Fe to what is now Mexico. Popé managed to unify the pueblos for a few years, but in 1692 the Spanish returned in what became known as the "peaceful reconquest."

Many of the returning Spanish behaved themselves and were better, less aggressive neighbors. Perhaps they had learned some humility and respect for those whose land they had taken. Today, many in the traditional Hispanic communities checkerboarding the area are related in one way or another to Pueblos, and the two cultures have shared lifestyles, food, music, and farming practices for generations.

Both cultures have also shared a suspicious view of the many waves of "newcomers" who have visited or settled in the valley. In the nineteenth century, the Santa Fe Trail and later the railroad opened New Mexico to Anglo merchants and settlers seeking escape, a quick buck, or a new life for whatever reason. Owing to folklore, pulp fiction, and undoubtedly some real experiences, they were fearful of the local Indians, probably not distinguishing between the different groups but seeing one brown, savage mass. Many had only a slightly more favorable view of the Spanish, describing with distaste in journals and letters the lifestyle, appearance, food, and dwellings of the Spanish settlers. Each new group seemed to bring with it a new layer of superiority based on the belief that they were the ones with the culture, the sophistication, and the civilized ways. And each wave of immigrants left another layer of resentment on those already here. Their goods and services may have been welcome, but their attitudes were not.

The early twentieth century brought lawyers, real estate speculators, and businessmen who colluded to change the balance of power in terms of landholdings. The Spanish had received large land grants for their communal use from the king of Spain, and these grants were confirmed by the US territorial government. But the law was no match for those who were determined to make a fortune, and the Spanish land grants fell victim to speculation, ending up in private hands. Subsequent waves of immigrants were drawn by the area's reputation for unspoiled nature, romantic and primitive peoples, and a simple lifestyle. And there were those escaping trouble elsewhere, some sent by wealthy families on both coasts who wanted them out of the way. Some of these became artists, writers, or eccentrics, adding to the area's reputation as a desirable and glamorous getaway. Today New Mexico has the romantic reputation as a utopia where the three cultures—Indian, Hispanic, and Anglo—live in harmony and have done so for centuries. That in itself is quite a tourist attraction. But the truth, of course, is far more complex.

Most recently have come the wealthy and weary, seeking beauty and solitude but bringing with them development and commotion. The Indians, the Hispanics, and anyone who has been in the area for a few decades may feel colonized once again by these newcomers with their golf courses, gated communities, swimming pools, and resorts. Ironically, the pueblos themselves, such as the Pueblo of Pojoaque, mentioned in the previous chapter, have become developers in much the same way, with casinos, golf courses, and resorts of their own. They want to support their people, grow the economy, and become players in the region. They are not willing to be kept in a museum, they say, for the viewing pleasure of tourists. The layers of complexity make for a very rich landscape and one on which the newcomer must tread carefully.

Thanks to my experience at the library meeting and soul-searching discussions with several Hispanic and Native colleagues from rural communities, we at Western Network began to learn about our backyard, and we tried to act responsibly. We adopted a policy that ensured our accountability to those we were working on behalf of. We made sure that they reviewed foundation proposals for accuracy, fairness, and their reflection of what was really needed. We included local community recipients in our funding proposals when appropriate, so that we could work together to make things better. And, looking within, we encouraged our office manager, Rosemary Romero, to move up the professional ladder. She was interested in the work we were doing, but she and we had assumed that she was relegated to the administrative side of things. After a series of staff meetings and retreats and much individual and institutional introspection, we all agreed that Rosemary was a natural mediator and facilitator and that there was no reason she shouldn't move right into a professional role. I became her mentor, and she was a great companion and co-worker. A native northern New Mexican, she brought a perspective and a commitment to community that enriched Western Network. Eventually she joined me and John as an equal partner.

Wanting to help more native New Mexicans break into our field, we applied for a grant that would enable us to hire two local Hispanic interns, Arón Rael and Richard Pacheco. The goal was to include them in all aspects of running a non-profit and to mentor them in mediation and facilitation. Our relationship became so close that we were unable to let them go at the end of the grant period, and they became invaluable associates. Our small staff was beginning to look more representative of the communities we were working with.

We decided that we also had a duty to try to educate members of the foundation community about the unintended consequences of their funding policies. If we had these connections with money, and if we were serious about ensuring that exploitation of local communities did not occur, then we should use our influence to enlighten the foundations. We discussed this with our program officer at the Ford Foundation, Walt Coward, and he responded positively. We agreed to convene a meeting in a few months so that he, and other foundation representatives, could sit with some of these community leaders who were critical of foundation grant-making choices in New Mexico.

It was no surprise that some community organizers made it clear that they would not come to a meeting organized by entremetidos who were acting as "gatekeepers" to the foundations. We arranged for Walt to invite them directly, but there was still suspicion in some camps that Western Network was behind it and that this was just one more way of using local people—parading them in front of funders to enhance our own credibility. It was frustrating, but we were determined.

The meeting took place the next spring in a neutral location, La Posada de Santa Fe, under a huge apricot tree on the hotel's lawn. Present were representatives of fourteen local communities and grassroots organizations and four foundations. The mood was serious and respectful but with an underlying tension. The foundation people introduced themselves and described briefly the focus of their funding. The community and grassroots representatives spoke eloquently about their needs and their lack of success with grant applications. They described the stresses on their staff, the lack of capacity in many administrative areas, and the pressures they felt from those they were trying to help. The foundation representatives were receptive and thoughtful. Walt Coward was particularly frank about the dilemma of those staffing large foundations, with thousands of decisions to make each year and many miles between themselves and the applicants.

"We simply don't have the information to make choices among dozens of competing applications in the same region," he said. He explained it was impossible to evaluate the credibility, the appropriateness, the feasibility of each proposal. But he had an idea. The Ford Foundation, and perhaps others, could make a significant grant each year for a certain number of years to the New Mexico Community Foundation (NMCF), to be granted in turn to local organizations as the NMCF saw fit. The NMCF could provide an application and selection process that would be open and accountable to the communities, funded and not funded.

The response was mixed. Some trusted the NMCF. Some preferred a direct relationship with the primary foundation and saw the NMCF as another gatekeeper between the grantees and the money. But all expressed appreciation for the time and the thoughtfulness that the foundations gave to the communities and their problems. And it was clear, from the interactions during lunch after the meeting, that connections were made and some level of comfort existed on both sides. The Ford Foundation followed through and included New Mexico in a multiyear pilot project that granted money to state community foundations for regranting to smaller applicants.

Shortly after the meeting under the apricot tree, Western Network made the decision to shift from foundation funding to a fee-for-service arrangement, wherein the clients would pay for our work. We had tried our best to be responsible grantees, but there was always that accountability question hanging over us. If we were successful in gaining foundation funding, yet no real client in the real world would pay us for what we were doing, wouldn't that be a pretty clear message to begin looking for another career? In the most clinical light, we were interested in what we were worth.

We set a goal for ourselves. In two years we would cut our foundation funding in half, and in five years we would wean ourselves entirely. We met our goals, I'm glad to say, although in the long run Western Network was not sustainable, and in 1999 we parted ways to hang out our own shingles. The stories in chapters 1 through 8 of this book are from the Western Network era; those in chapters 9, 10, and 11 are from my years in private practice. They all show that the reward of conflict resolution work is measured by more than income.

CHAPTER THREE

The Power of Story

When I was born, my father ran out of the hospital and headed straight for his suburban garden on the outskirts of Seattle. I assume he gave me a decent welcome into the world, a beaming smile, a little male-style coo of some kind, and a brief holding of my sturdy little newborn body. But he had a special job to do. It was April. His garden was on his mind, and he didn't want to waste a minute.

In those days, new mothers stayed in the hospital a luxurious amount of time, up to two weeks for a normal delivery. My mother enjoyed every minute of it and still talks about the divine taste of those scrambled eggs every morning, the kind nurses who educated her about how to care for her first baby, and the marvel of her little Lucy, with jet-black hair and chubby, red cheeks.

After ten days, my father brought us home. But before he allowed my mother in the house, he led her to his garden. With me in her arms, she rounded the corner of the house and saw a freshly spaded and planted area. She has told me over the years, every time with tears in her eyes, "And there was the name 'Lucy' planted in radishes. He had planted the seeds to spell 'Lucy' the day you were born, and they were just popping up, so new, so fresh—just like you."

It is a story that I have always loved. It says something about my father, my mother, and me, who we were, how we felt about one another, what it was like back then. And, of course, I like it because it is the first story about me. It is also a "naming story." Many cultures have rituals for naming new babies, and thanks to my father I have my own story of my naming. Had my babies been born in the right season, and in a fertile land, I might have followed in his footsteps and created a tradition, but that was not the case. And so I keep it as my own first story.

For me as a mediator, it is all about the story. Each of us is made up of our stories—stories about our ancestors, our childhoods, crises that have changed our lives, moments of insight and inspiration. A story that sticks with the listener has drama and somehow inspires, or at least offers a new view of the world. It draws you in, and you imagine that you are one or more of those characters. What would I do in that situation? Would I be that brave? That foolish? That creative? You might carry a message with you from the story, and if it is a powerful one you may be a slightly different person because of it. You may be captivated and convinced, or repelled and defensive, but you cannot help but be touched if the teller is honest, sincere, and perhaps vulnerable. In any case, you have a relationship with the teller that you did not have before. And for sure, the story will stick with you, whereas a paragraph like this one—a lecture of sorts—will quickly fade.

I have seen the impact a story can have on a group struggling to find common ground, and I am always amazed at the courage some people have to open up and tell those stories. One of my earliest experiences came in Denver in 1992.

I had been called by the director of the National Association of Counties (NACo) to bail the group out of a very tough situation. Headquartered in Washington, DC, NACo is a powerful lobbying organization dedicated to the well-being of counties and their officials and employees throughout the United States. The membership includes all elected county officials in the country—sheriffs, clerks, commissioners, and so on. A small percentage of NACo members also happen to be members of Indian communities, reservations, and nations, since many counties, especially in the western United States, include Indian lands within their borders.

The overlapping jurisdictions of tribes and counties had become a point of contention in the late 1980s and early 1990s. It was too difficult, said county leadership in Wisconsin, Washington, and Utah, among other states, to try to serve county citizens when a significant piece of the county's land base was reservation land. Expected to serve all citizens, including tribal members, they claimed the counties were denied taxation, law enforcement, and regulatory authority on Indian land. Furthermore, and this was particularly irritating, some tribes were beginning to compete with local government, setting up businesses, attracting county dollars to casinos, and levying their own taxes on county citizens. It was time for Native Americans to leave their entitlements behind, said these county officials, and become "regular citizens." The disgruntled counties pressured NACo to initiate legislation that would abrogate treaties with tribes.

The reaction from the tribal membership of NACo was swift. This was their organization, too, and they would not permit such a destructive initiative to be considered. A serious schism developed between the Indian and non-Indian members of NACo, and in response the organization formed a task force on county and tribal government relations. The task force was mandated to resolve the tough issues—treaty rights and the county-tribal relationship—and draft policy recommendations for the NACo board that would guide the organization's future actions with respect to tribes and counties. The twelve task force members (six Indian and six non-Indian) were to deliver the results of their negotiations at the annual NACo meeting the following month.

My job was to mediate the task force's final meeting, its last chance to reach consensus on how the organization should deal with "Indian issues." The group had met five times in ten months, to no avail. In the meeting minutes I saw diatribes from both sides: "You don't know what it's like to try to run a county that includes Indian land. It's not fair." "You don't understand our history as Native peoples and the meaning of tribal sovereignty." For all the presentations, legal arguments, and emotional pleas from both sides, neither message was getting through. The group was at an impasse. It was a predictable, but very sad, situation. I drove for seven hours from Santa Fe to Denver, praying that the road would reveal a bright idea to break the impasse. No such luck.

As I walked into the hotel meeting room and saw those twelve weary faces, I was filled with empathy and anxiety. I have learned that this is not necessarily a bad pair of emotions for a first encounter. Empathy allows me to connect with people at an emotional level, and anxiety keeps me on my toes and humble. In this case, my anxiety was not free-floating but had a very real basis. How could I help this exhausted group find a more constructive path? In an effort to buy time, and still hoping for divine inspiration, I suggested that each of them introduce himself or herself. "Of course," I said, "you all must know each other well by now, but I am new here. So, for my sake, please take your time and tell me a little bit about yourself." I thought this might take a half hour or so. It would allow me time to get a feel for the group and, I hoped, make a plan.

The first two participants, both Anglos, went quickly, rattling off their home areas, their professions, their relationships to their county. "I'm Joe Jameson from Vernal, Utah. I own the feed store, and I'm the county clerk." "My name is Sally Burnett. I'm a housewife and county commissioner in Snohomish County—that's in Washington State." Oh no, I thought, this is going to be over too soon. I panicked. There would be no time to plan my next step.

But I needn't have worried. The next task force member was a Hopi woman from Navajo County, Arizona. Her name was Thelma, and she began slowly.

"I was born just outside Holbrook—do you know where Holbrook is?" She looked around the table at the eleven blank faces. "Well, it's about in the middle of the state of Arizona, about fifty miles south of Oraibi, where my family lived. My dad was driving as fast as he could to get to the hospital, but he didn't make it, and I was born in the pickup just north of Holbrook," she said with a chuckle. She continued, in chronological order, with the highlights of her life, including cultural footnotes along the way. "My grandma really raised me and my four sisters—that's the way a lot of us were raised." She gave us a picture of Hopi life in the villages. "I was really busy when the melons came in—that was the time when the men danced their ceremonial dances and the women and girls did a lot of cooking, special kinds of food." She even gave us a recipe for the paper-thin blue corn piki bread, explaining how it must be cooked on a hot stone to be authentic. She told us about her favorite dog and its demise under her uncle's pickup, about her homesick days in boarding school, about the pain of her mother's alcoholism, and about her struggle to get through high school.

By the time she was twenty-four she had four small children, no job, and a husband who was gone most of the time, working on the railroad. And then, just when things were really bleak, she received word that her husband had been killed. They claimed he had been drinking and had passed out on the tracks, but she never believed that. "He wasn't a drinker," she said with certainty. "Not him. He was a good man. But what could I do? Now I was a widow with four little children, still with no job and now with no husband."

Early on in this saga, I began to get nervous. After five minutes, she was still at the elementary boarding school outside Tuba City. At ten minutes, she was spending a summer with a Navajo cousin, herding sheep. (Late one afternoon, their flock was attacked by coyotes and they lost three lambs, and they almost lost their best sheepherding dog, too.) At fifteen minutes, her fourth child was born. (She named her Darrelyn, after her husband, Darrel.)

I had a silent conversation with myself. Should I interrupt her and move the introductions along? That would be the fair thing to do, making time for the others. But it was a riveting story, and she was so generous in her offering of it, and, after all, Native Americans value a good story. I looked around the table for a cue and saw eleven faces mesmerized like mine. I sat back and listened.

She was at a turning point, she said. Her sister stepped in and helped with the children, or she never could have done what she did. She went to the community college! She beamed as she told us about the experience and her pride in getting her associate degree as an alcoholism counselor. She worked for the state program and began to see how government could help or hurt someone struggling for a better life. She wished that the local government in Navajo County took more interest in the Hopi citizens. A friend convinced her to run for a seat on the county commission. She thought at first it was an impossible idea, that being an elected official was what white people did, not a little Hopi lady. She laughed at the memory of her grandchildren holding signs for her along the highway, where one car passed every half hour. She told how she felt when she heard she had won, the first Hopi ever elected to county office. "And I was a woman, too!" she said, beaming.

"Then," she said, "came the scariest moment in my life." What on earth was coming next? We had heard terrifying moments from her life:

when the snake bit her baby sister, when her mother died in jail, when she was widowed at twenty-four, when her oldest son was missing in the mountains for three days. What could be scarier? We were on the edges of our seats.

She went on. "I walked into the commission meeting room on that first night, and I looked at those huge leather chairs, you know, where the commissioners sit." She scanned the faces of the other county officials sitting at the table and smiled in a quizzical way. "Why do they make those chairs so big? Do you know what I mean? They are so big!"

The others smiled and chuckled, saying, "Yeah, you're right," and "I don't know why they make them so big," or just nodded in acknowledgment.

"Well, anyway, my chair looked extra big that night, and I was so scared. I thought, 'What am I doing here, a little old Hopi lady? That big chair's not for me.' But you know what I did? I walked up to that chair—my knees were just shaking!—and I sat down! And now I've been sitting in that chair for three terms. I'm not scared anymore. I like being a county commissioner, and I try to do a good job for everyone in the county—not just the Hopis—I help the whites, too, and even the Navajos!" she said with a laugh. "Well, that's my story," she said, "and I sure appreciate you listening to me."

I looked around the table. There were smiles; there were looks of admiration; there were some moist eyes. I thanked Thelma for her story and asked the next person to introduce herself. We continued around the table, hearing longer introductions from the Native Americans, but as we progressed the Anglo task force members began to open up, too, and reveal more of themselves. By the time we had completed the circle, it was almost time for lunch. Half the day was gone, and I was worried about the little time remaining to deal with the tough issues.

But I was also worried about Joe Jameson and Sally Burnett, the first two elected officials whose introductions had been so abbreviated. It felt incomplete. I had learned that if something like that is haunting me, refusing to be pushed aside, I need to give it attention. And so I asked them if they would like to elaborate a little bit on their introductions. They looked both relieved and nervous and seemed to welcome the chance to offer more of themselves to the group. Sally spoke more about her family, including a covered-wagon vignette from her great-grandmother. Joe told briefly but powerfully about the loss of his son in a drowning accident and how that had influenced some his choices about the rest of his life. Sensing that the group felt complete now, I suggested that we adjourn to eat lunch together in the hotel dining room and come back at 1:30 p.m. to address the problems before us.

When the task force members returned from lunch, it was clear that the group had found a level of relaxation, even affection in some cases, that had not existed before. I feared that this atmosphere would fall victim to the hostilities that I was sure lay ahead. But I was in for a surprise.

The members had no trouble seeing the path they needed to take. The old hostility and resentment had been replaced by compassion and understanding. The mood was calm, the way was clear. They agreed that there was no decision, or rule, that was going to apply in all situations involving counties and tribes.

"After this morning, and hearing all those stories," concluded a sheriff from Montana, "it's clear to me that every situation with a tribe and county is different. Each county is different. Each tribe is different, and the way it all fits together is going to be different."

Another Anglo conceded, "Dissolving treaties is out of the question. I can see that's not going to happen. There's too much history there." The point, they saw, was to find a way to work together on a site-by-site basis, getting together, listening, learning, finding ways to improve the lives of county citizens and tribal citizens alike. That would be their recommendation to NACo's board of directors next month. Together, they developed steps that NACo might take to help in these individual situations, and it was a challenge for me to write their ideas fast enough on the flip chart. By this time I was using a purple marker (the black and blue ones had given out), and this list of ideas became the "Purple List." The Purple List included ways that NACo could serve as a clearinghouse and a resource for technical assistance to counties dealing with tribal issues. Members also wanted the Purple List to include a communications function for NACo whereby the organization could disseminate success stories and lessons learned from those areas where counties and tribes share overlapping territory. NACo, they said, should improve the quality and distribution of its newsletter and should hold special workshops and conferences on the subject of tribal-county relations. The task force urged NACo not to hide from these tough issues but to take a leadership role and show how they could be handled successfully.

As I remember it, we even finished early that afternoon. The task force co-chairs had instructions from their colleagues and were ready to deliver the Purple List to the annual NACo conference the following month in Florida. The group dissolved into twos and threes and straggled out of the room. The good-byes were sincere; the exclamations of "See you next month" were warm. I stayed until the last member had left the room, packed up my markers, rolled up my flip chart papers, and took a last look at the hollow-square table arrangement, site of such a remarkable event.

I drove home, flying along the highway, high on the life story and its impact on the group. It felt like a miracle. I had let go of the process and allowed a ridiculous amount of time (by Anglo standards) for introductions, and it had worked. I had adjusted the process to accommodate the cultural differences in the room, and we had reached some kind of breakthrough in which it all came together. I reported on my success to my colleagues at Western Network. They were as transfixed by my story as I had been by the Hopi grandmother's narrative. We talked about the power of such a story to bridge cultural barriers within a group. Stories were indeed powerful tools, and I was going to be sure to remember that.

A few weeks later, I found myself in the conference room at the Pueblo of Sandia. The pueblo is surrounded by developed land, bounded by Albuquerque to the south, Bernalillo to the north, Rio Rancho to the west, and, blessedly, the Sandia Mountains to the east. The pueblo's survival has depended on the residents' ability to protect their land and resources from the cities pressing up against their borders. This has required a strong government, a deep sense of community, and good negotiating skills. In addition, Sandia Pueblo wanted to make its own economic future secure in order to be able to keep predatory neighbors at bay. The tribal council had formed the Sandia Pueblo Economic Development Committee to create a five-year plan for the pueblo, and I had been asked to facilitate a one-day meeting of this committee. The members needed my help to explore several potential scenarios for future development, and I looked forward to working with them.

The ten committee members filed in and took places at the tables arranged in a U shape. I was at the open end of the U, with flip chart and markers, ready for action. I was surprised by the diversity of the group. I had anticipated Anglos and Sandia Pueblo members, but there were also an African American man, an Asian American woman, a man who seemed East Indian or Pakistani, and a woman who looked more Apache than Pueblo to me. I concluded that this would be an ideal situation in which to use my newfound telling-your-life-story tool.

I began by saying how pleased I was to be able to help the pueblo with its economic development strategy, and then, just as I had with the county-tribal task force in Denver, I said, "You probably know each other, but I am a stranger here, and I would appreciate it if you could introduce yourselves." I urged them to take more than the usual ten seconds, explaining that it was important for a group to really know something about one another before settling down to work. I looked expectantly at the multicultural faces before me. They were blank. Maybe the pump needed priming, I thought, and I offered to go first.

Taking silence as a mandate, I plunged ahead. I began with my birthplace in Seattle, the profession of my father, my mother the homemaker, and my two cats, Kitty and Buster, and how much I had loved them. I told about the importance of reading in my early years, the loneliness of being an only child. I moved quickly through my college years but dwelt on the years I spent on the Navajo reservation, my close friends there, my struggles with the Navajo language, my tenure as justice of the peace. And then on to Santa Fe, where I made wooden toys for a year, was a paralegal on a big uranium antitrust case, and then joined Western Network. I said that I loved my work and, again, was "delighted to be able to spend the day at Sandia with all of you . . ." I thought about five minutes had gone by, but when I looked at the clock I realized it must have been nearer fifteen. There would still be plenty of time for the others, who I hoped were inspired by my modeling of the life story.

I turned to the first person on my right, inviting him to introduce himself. He was a Sandia Pueblo councilman with a degree in economics from the University of New Mexico, and he was serving as chair of the committee. Period. That was it. I paused, wondering whether to ask for more, but chose not to be pushy. I turned to the next person. The African

American man smiled weakly, stated his name, and said that he was originally from Cleveland and now was a planner for the pueblo. Period. Next person. The man from India made a joke about being the "other kind" of Indian and said he had been in the United States for ten years and worked at the pueblo as an environmental technician. Period. It was like that, one after the other. They completed their introductions—all of them—in four minutes. The last person, on my immediate left, a woman from the pueblo, added, with a pointed look in my direction, "I wear three different hats at the pueblo, and it is hard to find time to do everything. We really have a lot of work to do today."

By this time, the message needed no punctuation. The members of this group were not interested in life stories. They had work to do, and they had hired a facilitator to help them do it. I had made a fool of myself. I struggled through the day, trying to redeem myself by being the most excellent facilitator they had ever seen. But I know that their lasting memory was not of my skills but of my life story. I know they left wondering what on earth had possessed that woman to tell her life story to the Sandia Pueblo Economic Development Committee.

What effective teachers those mistakes are. I never, ever again made the assumption that I had the answer to dealing with a cross-cultural group. Each one is different, and each one will have its own ways. It is up to me to be flexible enough to let those ways evolve. I still blush at the thought of that day at Sandia.

CHAPTER FOUR

Sheep in the Wilderness

The sheep thought they'd gone to heaven. Antonio feared he was headed in the other direction. It was the night of August 17, 1989, and he, his wife, Molly, and sheepherder Martín were driving over 1,100 mothers and their lambs under a full moon onto the William A. Humphries Wildlife Management Area without a permit. Antonio knew the country well. He'd had many adventures growing up in these northern New Mexico mountains, hunting, camping, fishing. But those adventures seemed very far away, and very innocent, compared with what lay ahead. He was committing criminal trespass, and the responsibility weighed on him heavily. They would be judged as heroes or fools, depending on how things turned out.

He picked a place where the fence was down and the animals could cross without danger. Cattle and weather had pushed rotted fences over, and, ironically, the sheep were met by several cows already munching on the lush grass in the promised land. Molly brought up the rear. Like her husband, she was worried about the consequences of their actions, but her main concern was their four children. Staying with her parents, they were safe, of course, but she missed them and wondered what effect her decision would have on them.

Villagers of the Rio Chama Valley, in the mountains of northern New Mexico, have been raising sheep for generations, but it is a tradition that has suffered in recent decades. The opportunities and seductions of nearby towns and farther-away cities have siphoned off most of the young adults who would have become the community's herders of the future. They chose a steady job and an easier lifestyle over the rural hardships of their youth. By the 1980s, the 25 percent unemployment rate and population drain were threatening to turn Los Ojos into a ghost town.

But there were those, both native to the area and newcomers, who did not want to let that happen. Antonio Manzanares, a college graduate with a bachelor's degree in psychology, chose to return home and try to make a living raising sheep. Maria Varela, a savvy community organizer fresh from civil rights work in Mississippi, was invited by land-grant activists to bring her skills to northern New Mexico. She helped start a badly needed health clinic in 1969 and learned from community members and doctors what Antonio already knew—economic stress and poverty were at the root of many of the medical problems in the Chama Valley. Was there a way, the two wondered, to turn this situation around?

In 1983, in an inspired and radical move—and after years of planning—Maria, Antonio, and teacher and fellow rancher Gumercindo Salazar joined with several Chama Valley families to form Ganados del Valle (Flocks of the Valley), a woolgrowers' organization that eventually became a non-profit. With a vision of merging cultural assets and sound business practices, they were committed to keeping ancestral lands in agriculture and lowering the poverty rate. (The effort eventually included other enterprises, including a lamb-marketing business and an arts and crafts center.) Ganados incubated Tierra Wools, a spinning and weaving operation that brought back the Churro sheep, renowned for its fine weaving wool. By 1989, Tierra Wools was employing twenty-five people and selling $200,000 worth of woven goods per year.

But a basic problem remained. The sheep—fundamental to this effort—needed grazing land in the summer. In the winter, when the pastures and mountain meadows were covered in snow, Antonio and other ranchers kept the sheep penned up and fed them hay. But in the spring they used traditional practices, pooling their sheep and driving them collectively to pasture in the high grasslands surrounding the valley for the summer. While the sheep were away, the ranchers could grow hay to harvest in the fall for winter feed. As Tierra Wools grew, so did the flocks, and every year it was a nightmare for the ranchers to find land and a permit to graze. The US Forest Service, the New Mexico Department of Game and Fish, and others with large pastures were raising rates, and Ganados was getting squeezed out.

In 1986, the Ganados leadership sought help from congressional staff and the governor's office. They argued that, if successful, their ventures would keep agricultural land productive, increase income for sheep-raising families, and provide new jobs. Senator Pete Domenici made a visit, as did Robert Redford, with no results. Without summer pasture, flocks would have to be sold, the nearly extinct Churro sheep would be at risk, and the fledgling economic development experiment would disappear.

Particularly frustrating to the community was the fact that the herders were being denied access to traditional common lands of the Tierra Amarilla Land Grant. (As we saw in chapter 2, this is another example of the importance of understanding the landscape, in all senses, of any conflict.) The 600,000-acre land grant had been deeded by the Mexican government in 1832 to Spanish settlers in the area. The intention, and the practice for generations, was to use the undivided area for grazing valley residents' flocks in common. Through some legal maneuvering in the late 1800s the land moved into private hands, and in the 1900s it began to pass from one owner to the next. In spite of the ownership status, local ranchers continued to graze their flocks until the 1940s, when new owners fenced the once-common land.

The Edward Sargent Wildlife Management Area was in the sights of Ganados. For decades it had been owned by Edward Sargent, the biggest sheep rancher around. Small local ranchers were familiar with the property—high in the mountains, with plenty of water—because they often leased a flock to manage for Sargent, giving him 30 percent of the wool and lamb revenue. So it made sense to Antonio and company that when the property was sold to The Nature Conservancy in 1975, and then donated to the New Mexico Department of Game and Fish, it would be available for grazing. In fact, grazing was permitted as a forage management tool, and the commission leased some of the property back to the former owner for cattle grazing.

For several years the Ganados folks lobbied the governor and the New Mexico Game and Fish Commission (decision makers for the department) for permits to graze, but the hunting and conservation interests argued successfully against them. They reminded the commission that The Nature Conservancy stipulated management of the resource "for the benefit of wildlife," and in their opinion sheep and wildlife were not compatible. Although environmental interests had early on supported Ganados as a model of sustainability, even buying the organization's first guard dogs, they now quietly lobbied against them. When the Ganados leadership realized they were being undermined behind the scenes, they were disappointed. "We saw that the deck was stacked against us," said Antonio.

In the spring of 1989, Ganados negotiated with the Jicarilla Apache Nation for rights to graze their sheep on El Poso Ranch, marginal grazing land but Ganados's only option. In late July, the nation sent a letter revoking the permit because of pending litigation with the state. Ganados was given two weeks to vacate. With the summer disappearing and no other permit in sight, the organization met to consider its options. After a long, difficult meeting, fourteen frustrated and desperate Ganados families agreed to a "sheep-in," but only on condition that the authorities would never know who owned the lawbreaking animals. Although the Sargent was their property of choice, it was too distant for the quick action they needed. So they turned to the William A. Humphries Wildlife Management Area, which had much the same history as the Sargent. It was drier, but being adjacent to El Poso, at least it was accessible.

With the sheep hidden in the Humphries, Ganados leadership held a press conference on August 18 to announce the action. The announcement hit like a bomb. The law had been broken. Hunters, recreationists, and taxpayers were angry that this renegade band of sheepherders had been so presumptuous as to move their sheep onto public property. But more enraged were environmentalists, who felt they had a moral and legal obligation to protect that property from the ravages of grazing. They were sure that The Nature Conservancy's conditions on the property did not include sheep in the definition of wildlife to be benefited. They pushed the governor to take immediate action against the offending animals and their herders.

Surely in the back of Governor Garrey Carruthers's mind was the raid and occupation of the courthouse at Tierra Amarilla in 1967. The raid's leader, Texas-born Reies López Tijerina, had moved to Arizona as a fundamentalist preacher. He had done copious research on Spanish and Mexican land grants, and once relocated in Tierra Amarilla he applied his considerable charisma, knowledge, and energy to reclaiming those lands to benefit the local economy. His movement, La Alianza Federal de Mercedes (the Federal Land-Grant Alliance), gained a strong and passionate following. Supporters held protest marches in Albuquerque and Santa Fe and occupied a park near Tierra Amarilla, but to no effect. After a district attorney prohibited him from organizing a public meeting in northern New Mexico, Tijerina and a handful of followers went to the courthouse to make a citizen's arrest of the district attorney for violation of their constitutional rights. There was a shoot-out, leaving a jailer and a deputy wounded. The band kidnapped a deputy and a court reporter but soon released them. Tijerina received a two-year sentence for assault. The incident brought national attention to this corner of the Wild West. Locally, it was a wake-up call to those in power that the region was seething with discontent.

And in case the authorities had pushed the snooze button, the alarm went off again in 1988, when Amador Flores and his family sought to reclaim land he had paid taxes on under the doctrine of adverse possession. Flores and his followers set up an encampment, with bunkers and barricades, by the highway just outside Tierra Amarilla. The land belonged at the time to Vistas del Brazos, an Arizona-based land investment firm, and Flores and his family were demanding its return to the community. They were successful and received a cash settlement as well as acreage, now communally owned. But just as a reminder, a homemade billboard still stands at that spot on the highway. Handwritten in big, bold, black letters at the top is "Tierra o Muerte."

Both the courthouse raid and the later occupation attracted national attention for months, so it was no wonder that Governor Carruthers acted with restraint when he was told of the occupation of the wildlife management area by Chama Valley natives. Hoping to avoid another front-page story, he was deliberately slow to respond, trying to buy time for a resolution to the explosive situation. But the Ganados press conference had stirred up a hornet's nest, and members of the environmental community were outraged. They held their own press conference demanding action from the governor—even calling out the National Guard—to protect the state's wildlife and prosecute the criminal trespassers.

In the meantime, the sheep hardly had to move to fill themselves on the lush mountain grass, but Antonio, Molly, and Martín kept them trotting deeper into the trees, hoping for cover from the planes they knew would be looking for them. Gumercindo, now Ganados board chair, drove supplies in to a drop-off point, careful not to be spotted. His heart was with the trespassers, but he and many others were afraid of losing their jobs if they participated openly. The three spent a chilly but pleasant night under a sky with stars that seemed to be leaping toward them, they were so brilliant. They ate sandwiches, not wanting to draw attention with a fire, and slept in bedrolls on the ground. They had no idea what to expect, but they knew that their days, maybe hours, were numbered. Sooner or later, they would be found and brought out.

On the second day of the "sheep-in," the governor sent a state plane to fly over the area. The sheep were spotted around midday. Martín looked at the sky nervously. "Wow, that's a lot of planes," he observed, thinking that the single plane going back and forth was a whole squadron flying over. This brought a much-needed laugh. They knew they could not hide the sheep, so they decided to try to make their band of three appear to be more numerous. They changed their hats and turned their jackets inside out and kept moving, hoping to seem more formidable than they really were. They laughed in spite of the uncertain future as they tried to figure out ways to multiply the horses in the same way they were multiplying the people. "We should've brought wigs for the horses," said Antonio, "or covered them in Naugahyde or something."

They hadn't talked about what might happen next, but it had to be on their minds. They were worried about the consequences of breaking the law and hoped that the authorities would be gentle with them. As leader of the pack, Antonio realized that he might go to jail, and he hoped that it would be in Tierra Amarilla rather than in Santa Fe, where he would be seen as a troublemaking sheepherder. Of equal concern was the reaction of their neighbors in the Chama Valley. There were villagers who supported the action because of the weaving and other jobs that Ganados had created, but there were others who felt it was a reckless move that would only bring more trouble to the community, just another embarrassment like Tijerina or Flores. Antonio was no Tijerina or Flores, but he knew that he and the others were risking credibility among some in the community, and that troubled him. Worried about her children, who had just started school, Molly wished she could be with them to deal with the usual crises of classes, clubs, and wardrobe. She secretly hoped that they would all be herded out soon. Martín was worried about the planes.

Back at Tierra Wools, Maria met with the weavers to talk about how to support the effort. Molly was one of their own, and they felt for her and appreciated the risk she was taking. They knew that the weavers, as well as the sheep owners, had a vested interest in the action. Weighing carefully the possibility of arrest and jail, two weavers decided to join her. Maria continued dealing with the media and pressuring the governor's office to find grazing land for the rest of the summer.

But the governor was getting pressure from other quarters to arrest the desperadoes and bring them to justice. On the third day, seven officers from the New Mexico Department of Game and Fish appeared from behind the small hills surrounding the camp. Armed and on horseback, they reminded Antonio of the Magnificent Seven riding into town. Two came forward, dismounted, and extended greetings. One was a good friend, sympathetic to the cause. He asked the three politely to leave with their sheep, and Antonio answered that he could not make that decision alone. The officer issued a trespassing ticket and turned to remount his horse but found that it had disappeared, probably for a quick meal of sweet grass. Molly had to ride out and bring the horse back. The officer thanked her kindly and rode off.

That afternoon, Antonio rode out to a prearranged place to meet Maria and review their strategy. She reported that the governor had appointed a special advisor to find state land for the sheep nearby. He just needed more time, Maria said, and she asked Antonio to stay one more day until the deal was sealed. The next day Molly, Martín, and several weavers and flock owners drove the sheep back along the road, wanting to be in the open as much as possible, still fearing repercussions. Antonio was afraid that nothing positive would come from the action and that the community would turn on him and his family. But he arrived to a largely supportive community and good news. Maria reported that the governor had made available Heron Lake State Park for three weeks of grazing, just enough time for flock owners to harvest winter feed and bring the sheep back to home pastures. But this was an emergency measure that could not be used again next year.

Ganados grazers warned that the same thing would happen the next season without a permanent solution, and for lawbreakers, they were attracting a great deal of positive attention outside their own boundaries. There was sympathy for this community that was trying to pull itself up by the bootstraps. There was also growing hostility in the rural West against the environmental movement. Maria was an effective hispana spokesperson; Antonio was a charismatic hispano rancher; and those lambs—what could be cuter than those lambs?

David Henderson, state director for Audubon New Mexico, confided to me shortly after the first publicity on the subject, "I'm not used to this. We're the ones with the pictures of appealing animals. We're the ones defending the baby seals in the Arctic from the bludgeoning hunters. And here we are, painted like the bad guy, and on the other side is a little girl holding a baby lamb." He was reacting to a half-page photo and accompanying article in the New York Times describing the situation and outlining the conflict. The picture gave a clue to which side had the upper hand in the public arena. The rights of the rural Hispanic community to use its traditional land clearly prevailed over the rights of environmentalists and state government to defend that land, now public domain, for the use of wildlife and to the exclusion of sheep.

The media attention was new for the community members, and uncomfortable as they may have been in the spotlight, they knew that they had better make the most of it. This was the time to establish their legitimacy in the arena of environmental decision making, and staking a claim to traditional communal lands was their strategy. They argued fiercely on moral, cultural, and scientific grounds. Sheep and elk, they said, are definitely compatible. Witness the healthy condition of the Sargent after decades of sheep grazing. Managing a wildlife refuge "for the benefit of wildlife" in fact could include sheep as a management tool, if the flock were carefully tended. This was a horrific idea to the environmentalists, who envisioned uprooted forage, trampled stream banks, and polluted water. The governor's task force, formed to find the answer before the question reappeared next summer, stumbled and stalled on the scientific issues.

Sheep were clearly either good or bad depending on whether you were a sheepherder or a wildlife lover, and both sides had scientists and studies to support them. The task force disbanded in early 1990, and the problem was left for the congressional delegation to pick up. The state had given the Ganados grazers a one-more-time-only permit to graze their sheep on state land again in the summer of 1990, but it was clear to everyone that a long-term solution had to be found.

In June, Senator Jeff Bingaman approached us at Western Network to see if mediation might be used to help solve the problem. He hoped to ensure that the still-explosive situation did not get any worse and that, come spring 1991, the Ganados sheep would have a secure pasture. He saw that the environmentalists and the sheep growers were locked in stalemate, and he hoped to find some common ground between the two—perhaps quite literally. We jumped at the chance to help, and, with foundation funding earmarked for cross-cultural work, we proceeded to assess the potential for a joint meeting.

We realized that the job needed a mediation team that reflected the makeup of the group we would be working with. I had experience with both Hispanic land-based communities and environmentalists, and for my partner I wanted Roberto Chené, a native New Mexican, trained as a counselor and a born mediator. We had met and worked earlier on a foundation project to explore ways Indians, Hispanics, and Anglo environmentalists could bridge cultural divides and form alliances for mutual benefit. It had been a wild, encounter-group kind of process, and I quickly saw his genius at dealing with volatile emotions. He could help people look at the roots of the conflict while calming their defensiveness, fear, and pain. I had complete confidence in his ability to handle this group. And he was—and is—a joy to work with.

With black, wavy hair, a round face, and green-gray eyes, he is a very appealing guy with a broad smile that he often flashes at his own expense. He also has a body type that can't quite keep up with his love of his native New Mexican food. Raised in the 1950s and 1960s, he knows intimately the impact of those waves of colonization and can relate to local minorities—hispano and Indian—who are overwhelmed by emotions they cannot identify or justify. He tells a wrenching story from second grade. Knowing that he walked to and from school, the teacher asked him one day if he passed the lumberyard on his way. A model student and eager to please, he said yes. She asked him to pick up a narrow board and bring it to her, "about this long," and she held her hands out a little wider than her shoulders. "And nice and strong," she added. He was excited to have such a grown-up assignment, and the next day he brought her a board that he hoped would make her happy. It turned out to be just perfect . . . for paddling a "bad boy" later that day. He was devastated to find that he had been made her accomplice and had betrayed his own classmate. That painful story, he says, was an example of oppression, helplessness, guilt, betrayal—so many of the elements found in conflicts between cultures. I learned from him that we all have known oppression at some time in our lives, most likely during childhood.

Roberto worked under contract to us at Western Network, and he (native hispano male) and I (outsider Anglo female) made a team that everyone—community members, newcomer environmentalists, men, women—could identify with. We were excited as we set up our first interviews with community leaders in Los Ojos and environmental leaders in Santa Fe. We hoped for enough support to move forward with a retreat of some kind, but we knew that if those we interviewed had no interest in coming together, there would be no next step. We asked ourselves and each other about our own biases. How did I feel as an Anglo and a relative newcomer (fourteen years) to the state? Did I have a Sierra Club membership card in my purse? Was that a problem? How did Roberto feel as a Hispano . . . with a French surname? How would they receive him in Los Ojos, when he was from Albuquerque? We agreed that it was important to stick together, to do all the interviews as a team. We wanted to have two perspectives on everything, and we wanted to demonstrate this multicultural model as we moved through the project, however short its life might be.

Antonio was first on our list. We drove up from Santa Fe, through the Española Valley and into the high-mountain Chama Valley. Sagebrush and chamisa were replaced with acres of green meadows. Snowcapped mountains to the west looked close enough to touch, and to the north the peaks jutted into the brilliant blue sky. We turned off the air-conditioning and rolled down the windows. The air was fragrant, balmy. We passed a painted wooden sign on our left declaring the sovereignty of the land-grant heirs, a last stand of the Flores occupation just two years earlier and a reminder of the hostility beneath this idyllic surface.

We took a dirt road a mile or so to the Manzanares house. Molly opened the door, a pretty woman with a serious face and a single long, brown braid down her back. She had on jeans and boots and a short-sleeved pink shirt. There was a quiet modesty about her that belied her accomplishments. I could see her riding next to Antonio, hustling those sheep into the wildlife area under the cover of night. It was also easy to see her baking bread and pies, slaughtering lambs, dyeing and spinning wool, weaving rugs, and raising children, all of which she did—and does—with a calm assurance. She went to retrieve Antonio from the back of the house.

He greeted us with handshakes and a hesitant smile. I felt he was looking us over, wondering what he was getting himself into, how long this was going to take, and who the hell we were. He had been reluctant to talk to us, but it seemed to impress him that we were willing to drive two hours north to his turf rather than ask him to make yet another trip down to the seat of power, Santa Fe. We exclaimed over the beauty of the day, and he reckoned as to how it was an unusually good one and asked if we would like to sit outside. So, happy as sheep in clover, Roberto and I slipped off our shoes and sat on the grass, picking blades and sucking the sweetness out of the stems. It was good to be outside, to be experiencing the land, the sky, the clean, fragrant air—all of which defined northern New Mexico.

We apologized for interrupting his day, acknowledging how busy he was. He graciously said he needed a break from the house repairs he had been working on, but we could tell he was overworked and under a lot of stress. Antonio is a handsome man with dark, thick hair and brown eyes, full lips, and perfect teeth. He has a gentle look, and like Molly he oozes competence. He seems to radiate a healthy rural way of life, a product of the generations of Manzanareses who have lived in that spot, supported by its abundance. A natural leader, he speaks for and on behalf of the community but without ego. He is passionate about his children and their futures and wants them to have every choice possible, whether it involves leaving or staying home. For him the choice is clear, and he will spend his life fighting for community rights, with the same passion as his more radical neighbors but using different strategies.

Antonio said he was ready to put the excitement of the previous August behind him and find a piece of land for next summer's flocks. And he was certainly not in a charitable mood toward the environmentalists, who had pressed for his arrest for trespassing on the wildlife management area. We talked for over an hour, shifting from one position to another. At times my attention wandered back to that incredible grass, so thick and hardy, so soft and supporting. I was intoxicated. I had been in the arid Southwest for more than twenty years, but those Seattle roots were still alive and thirsty for green grass. I kept gazing at the mountains, not far away, where Antonio had hidden the sheep and imagined the feast they must have had.

And then I realized that my mind was not really wandering; it was right on target. This conflict was all about this land, its resources, and its people. This piece of land, this gorgeous grass, the herd of sheep all belonged to the Manzanares family. Roberto and I were visiting. The Sierra Club was visiting. The New Mexico Department of Game and Fish was visiting. We were all visitors, with certain rights, but Antonio and his neighbors belonged here.

Roberto led the discussion. He asked Antonio about the history of Los Ojos, about his decision to raise sheep, about how he felt going onto the refuge in the middle of the night, and, finally, about his view of the environmental opposition. Antonio was feeling hopeless and angry, but most of all we felt his weariness. It was a huge struggle, and he didn't know if it was worth it, either on a personal level—with a family of six to support—or on a community level. Would he be willing to meet with some environmentalists, we finally asked, and talk about resolving this question about the compatibility of sheep and wildlife? He surprised me with a yes, although he added that he was probably crazy. And, he said, he was so busy and so worn out that it couldn't take a lot of time. We said we understood and we would make that our guiding principle for any next step. We thanked him for his time and his wisdom and, a little stiffly, stood up, leaving the grass with great reluctance. We said we would contact him after we had talked with environmentalists who had opposed his efforts, and maybe there would be some kind of joint session. He looked uncomfortable and shook his head as we shook hands. "I don't know. Hard to imagine," were his final words.

Next, we talked with David Henderson of the Audubon Society. We met in a coffee shop in Santa Fe, although I'm sure he, too, would have preferred that lush grass of Los Ojos. I thought about the symbolism of lounging in a meadow versus sitting on plastic chairs, hunched over a fake wood table. In a way, the coffee shop felt like my turf, where I "belonged." David was barely thirty, with light hair and mustache, blue eyes, and a long, lean build, perfect for the hiker, birder, rafter, and biker that he was. He had grown up in Southern California, had attended Humboldt State University in the 1970s, and confessed to being a hippie, but apparently one with a direction. He had majored in natural resources and environmental education, and when I asked him about his choice of wildlife as a focus, he said, laughing, "What's not to like about wildlife?" He added that it seemed to be a more controversial topic now that he was in New Mexico. He had come as state director for Audubon New Mexico three years ago and was thrilled by the six life zones here and the diversity of species—the greatest number of species of any state, everything from the prairie chicken to the ptarmigan. He was an energetic, youthful leader among environmentalists and had an easy way with all kinds of people. David was just plain likable. But it was obvious that he, like Antonio, was under stress. He laughed a little too nervously, a little too loud, and a little too often.

It was clear, he said, that the folks at Los Ojos had the upper hand and that the environmentalists were in an unfamiliar defensive position. In their efforts to preserve and protect resources for biodiversity, for wildlife, for recreation, and for the future, he and others were finding themselves facing an unexpected, and unexpectedly effective, opponent—the local community dependent on those resources, both economically and culturally. He was quick to criticize the trespass action but equally quick to say that he was not "anti-sheep." He was upset by the negative media coverage environmentalists were receiving and insisted on a media ban as a condition of any talks. He told us about his organization and its priorities and his personal interest in and commitment to the local natural resources. Land-based communities in northern New Mexico and environmentalists had so many enemies in common that he couldn't understand why they were at each other's throats. I sensed that he also took some responsibility for that situation and was willing to put effort into fixing it. With great discretion, he intimated that of course not all environmental organizations were the same and that there were those who might not be willing to meet with the locals.

Like Antonio, David described the demands on his time; running a non-profit, dealing with national leadership and a local board, and fund-raising were more than full-time, not to mention the frequent emergencies. But he understood that this conflict with Ganados del Valle was symbolic and saw that it could be a quagmire. In his campaigns to protect the Mexican spotted owl and to reintroduce the Mexican gray wolf, he had encountered other land-based communities who claimed his efforts were a direct threat to local livelihood and culture. He was bemused as he wondered aloud whether there might be another livelihood and culture that these ranchers and loggers had displaced not that long ago. How far back should you peel the layers to find the "legitimate" culture to be preserved, and at the bottom might you not find the natural landscape that he was fighting for? But he realized that, more than speculating, if he was going to be successful in New Mexico he needed to understand the current dynamics in the Chama Valley that motivated Ganados to take such extreme measures.

From these two interviews we took encouragement and moved on to interview other Ganados members and environmental leaders to test the feasibility of a meeting. The question, of course, was, "What for?" No one thought it possible to resolve the conflict between grazing and wildlife; the sides were too dug in. And the fact that they shared common enemies—developers, industry, mining, certain federal agencies—did not strike anyone as common ground on which to build a relationship. At the moment, each was the other's worst enemy. We backed up and asked if people would be willing to come together in a neutral, safe setting and see whether there was anything to talk about. Surprisingly, the answer was yes. There was curiosity about the "other" and a willingness to devote a discrete piece of time to the question "Is it worth it for me to try to have a relationship with any of these people?"

Both sides were tired of the battle and saw some dangerous handwriting on the wall. If they continued to fight each other, they might have nothing left for the bigger battle against those common enemies. At the very least, they should stop opposing each other, even if an alliance were not possible. "Butting our heads together like two rams until one drops dead is no solution," declared a rancher. Perhaps not the most noble reason to enter into talks, this exhaustion and imminent defeat did serve as a real motivator.

The climate was ripe in other ways. Both sides were spending inordinate amounts of time, money, and staff energy on the battle. They were risking their reputations. The environmentalists were already suffering at the hands of the charismatic and photogenic sheepherding and weaving community. The community knew well, however, that the tide could turn against them, and that in fact there were plenty of New Mexicans—some within their own community—who resented their lawbreaking tactics. Perhaps individuals on both sides also saw the opportunity to be courageous and take a leadership role. Finally, I think each camp harbored a shred of hope that its side could convince the other of its rightness and thereby gain an important ally. "If we could just sit down together, away from the public eye, maybe they would listen to me and understand and even be converted."

With this tentative go-ahead, Senator Bingaman's office invited a group of ten, who had agreed to attend, to a three-and-a-half-day retreat on October 9–12, 1990, at Sol y Sombra in Santa Fe. Behind a huge wrought iron gate, Sol y Sombra was an elegant yet simple retreat center, complete with two acres of permaculture demonstration projects and constructed wetlands. At the request of Ganados, the owners, Beth and Charles Miller, had donated the use of the facility, including overnight rooms with organic cotton bedding and towels, and delicious organic food, much of it grown on the property. Supporters of both Ganados and environmental groups, they believed there had to be a way to bridge these differences.

The negotiated purpose and ground rules for the event were stated in the invitation. The five community members and the five environmentalists would "get acquainted, and would explore the potential for mutual trust." They would not discuss the issue of grazing. They would commit to listening and speaking with respect, and they would try to keep an open mind. The senator was extremely interested, he said, in fostering whatever relationships could be formed to increase understanding and minimize conflict. The stage was set.

Roberto and I knew that there were special needs in this situation. One was privacy. Although it is always important to provide a safe environment, with agreements about confidentiality, in this case it was crucial to the parties that there be privacy during the meetings and a ban on any reporting afterward. Both sides were taking a big risk and could be criticized by their constituents if word got out that they were sitting down with the enemy. This way, if the effort were a failure, no one would know that it had even been attempted.

There were also cultural and historical issues between the two groups. Like the acequia members in chapter 2, these villagers formed a traditional rural community hundreds of years old. The surrounding land and resources had supported them, economically, socially, and culturally, until waves of outsiders washed over the landscape. Without access to those resources, the heart of the community would die. This painful history, which predated by centuries the arrival of the environmentalists in question, was alive and relevant for those at Los Ojos. For them, the environmentalists were simply the latest wave of colonizers—white, educated, with access to money and powerful connections.

The environmentalists saw themselves as the good guys, arriving with knowledge and energy to protect the resources of this beautiful area. The area's complex history was remote and largely irrelevant to them. As Anglo Americans, they were mobile, detached or at least removed from roots and family, and enthusiastic about new frontiers. Preparing for these cultural differences, Roberto and I were grateful for each other's presence. "Lucy can handle those enviros," he thought, while I was counting on him to calm the community members.

Finally, it was very clear to us that this situation required the lowest of expectations and that if any progress were to be made, we would have to go very slowly and with great patience. We knew that this might be the first and last meeting of its kind and that we must rid ourselves of any expectations of glory or even appreciation. It could in fact be a disaster, in which case we would be very glad indeed that there had been no publicity.

The retreat began in the evening and was, inevitably, tense. As we were settling down in a comfortable meeting room, a Ganados member broke the ice with a comment about going through the wrought iron gate onto the property. Were they trying to keep us out or make sure we didn't get away? Another commented on the lush grass that carpeted the common area where the buildings faced. Could he arrange to have a few sheep brought down from Los Ojos, he asked. There were grateful laughs from all of us.

A spokesperson for the senator made some remarks, and Roberto and I introduced ourselves and tried to set a tone of optimism without expectations, which was tricky. After describing what we had learned in our interviews, we asked participants to introduce themselves and offer any hopes or expectations for their time together. That list, from both sides, included the following:

- To teach and to learn
- To do some difficult soul-searching
- To develop relationships and explore the possibility of trust
- To articulate the conflict together and face it head-on
- To reduce conflict and find common ground
- To let out anger and emotion
- To find a solution to the specific problem
- To satisfy curiosity about the process
- To have fun in a comfortable setting

And since we were creating lists, Roberto and I also asked for a list of ground rules. The group agreed by consensus to

- listen with respect,
- speak one at a time,
- avoid personal attacks,
- speak honestly and with "I" statements when possible,
- commit to work in good faith,
- be creative,
- set and keep time frames.

We facilitators were asked to enforce those rules and to identify common ground and clarify differences. It was an optimistic pair of lists, perhaps too optimistic. I was afraid that this might be a case of participants trying to say the right thing, trying to please the mediator. I needn't have worried. During the next day, we plunged in and wrestled with every one of the hopes and tested every one of the ground rules.

In the morning we asked the environmentalists and the community members to caucus separately and answer the following questions for themselves as a group:

- Who are we?
- What value does the land have for us, and how do we relate to it?
- What kind of understanding and support do we need from others?
- What parts of our struggle do we find difficult?

Then we brought the two groups together and asked each to "present" itself to the other side, in whatever format and at whatever length group members wanted. The listening side was to concentrate on listening, learning, and, we hoped, understanding. After the presentation, they could ask questions to clarify what they hadn't understood. The last step in the process gave the presenting side a chance to comment on the questions. Then it would be the turn of the other side to present.

The environmentalists presented first. They introduced themselves and gave brief autobiographies. It was clear that they were making an effort to reveal something about themselves that would be of interest to the community members and that would relate to their commitment to the environment. Some offered definitions of "environment" and "environmentalist"; some spoke about John Muir, Aldo Leopold, and other heroes; some described life-changing experiences they had undergone as they faced a particular challenge in nature. Their commitment was clear, as was their urgency. They felt that there was no time to waste, that the planet and its resources were facing increasing threats each day. It was important, they said, to look at this big picture and to understand that if we lose the planet, it won't matter whether or not there are sheep or elk in the wildlife management area. They identified with an environmental community, they said, not a geographic one, like Los Ojos, but a community of belief and commitment to common values.

During the question period, a weaver from Tierra Wools pressed an environmentalist. He had grown up in Pennsylvania somewhere, was that right? "Yes," he answered, "outside Philadelphia."

"Well," she said politely but pointedly, "I know where my land is, up at Los Ojos, but just where is your land?"

He responded, struggling, "I don't really have any land, not like you're talking about. I live in Santa Fe; that's where I live now." He hoped to bring the questioning to a close.

"But you came from there, in Pennsylvania. Isn't your family still there?"

"Sure, they're still there, my parents. They live in the same house where I grew up."

"And what does that land look like, where their house is? Is it nice?"

"Yeah, well, I guess so. It's like, you know, a suburb, just a street and houses and lots, small lots, with a little grass, you know. That's about it."

"But that's your land, your family's land?"

"Well, they own it . . ."

"So here's what I don't understand. You have land, your family's land, but you leave there, and I guess you don't want to go back there. What I don't understand is why you care so much about our land. You've got your own land." The implication, of course, was "And so why don't you go back to your land and leave us and our land alone?"

The environmentalist struggled to explain that the land in Pennsylvania was just a piece of property that you bought with a house on it and that he had never expected to stay there. He had left to go to college in the West and had fallen in love with the Rockies, and then, when he saw northern New Mexico with its pastures and peaks, he knew that was where he wanted to live. He was committed to New Mexico, wanted to raise his family here. He understood, he said, how she could be so attached to the land. He felt that way, too.

But this was not really true. The environmentalist's attachment to the land could not be the same, and during the Los Ojos panel presentation the differences became clear. The community members had organized their presentation so that each person spoke about a different aspect of the community—the economy, the culture and history, the connection to the land, the importance of sheep, the vision for the future. They also introduced themselves as individuals, but the focus of each presentation was on their role in the community and what the community meant to them. That land, which was genuinely appreciated by the environmentalists, was much more to the community people. It was a source of livelihood, of culture, of pride. It held treasures of their past and hopes for the future. Unlike much of the rest of America, these people were not going to move anywhere. The environmentalist might care for that same land, want to preserve it and protect it from degradation, but it was not his or hers in the same sense. It was a superficial attachment from the community's point of view and, given history, one to be wary of.

The community's presentation also raised issues of power. As poor, rural Hispanic villagers, they said, they had no power. They lacked education, connections, and money, and they felt powerless in the face of development, legal forces, and now environmental challenges. The environmentalists seized on what they saw as common ground. They were the ones without power fighting the dominant forces of industry and government. They were traditionally the underdogs, they tried to explain. And, now in fact, with respect to Ganados del Valle and Tierra Wools, the environmentalists were the ones without power. The "underdog" was destroying them in the media, and that was certainly a big source of power. The community members were quietly pleased to hear the enemy acknowledge their prowess. The environmentalists went on to ask why they seemed to be at the top of the community's enemy list when there were so many other, bigger enemies at the door.

"I'm a good guy," said one environmentalist. "You make me feel like some kind of Archie Bunker character who's racist and a jerk in every way. I just care about the environment—why is that so bad?"

A Ganados member responded. "It's your damn urgency that you lay on us, about the planet and how there's no time to lose. That scares me. Because when people with money and connections are in a hurry about something, that usually means it's going to happen. And in this case you are in a hurry to keep our sheep from grazing. Well, we're in a hurry, too. This is the last minute for our community and our way of life. If we can't find grazing land and make our organization work, we are lost. So, it might be nice to have the luxury of worrying about the planet in the next twenty years, but, hey, I'm worried about my family in the next six months."

Others added that this environmental ethic felt like another step in separating land from people. It rankled them that wildlife was the beneficiary of land and water resources in the eyes of these environmentalists while they and their children were not considered worthy of protection. And most insulting was the implication that the local people were not seen as competent stewards of areas they had managed for centuries, the very land that the environmentalists had fallen in love with because of its beauty.

By the end of that day, Roberto and I were exhausted but exhilarated. No one had walked out, in spite of some very tense moments. There had been laughter as well as tears. There certainly was a higher level of understanding between the two groups. And to top it off, we all gathered after dinner to drink beer, play poker, and look at the stars. People told stories from their childhood, exchanged insights about family dynamics, and told jokes at one another's expense. It was a remarkably congenial time. Things were looking up.

The plan was to take a field trip the next day to Los Ojos, a two-hour ride in a rented van. There were some last-minute objections from an environmentalist or two. It would take a long time. What was the point? And, finally, what about equal time for an "environmentalist field trip"? Would the group be willing to travel to Aldo Leopold's cabin near Tres Piedras or to the newly designated Wild and Scenic River up near the Colorado border? This gave us another chance to talk about different attachments to the land. For the community, there was only one piece of land that mattered, and on it depended their survival. For the environmentalists, there were dozens, hundreds of important places—important in an intellectual or philosophical or even spiritual sense—but not in a personal survival sense. The community held firm. If the environmentalists would not show the respect of traveling north, there was no point in continuing to talk. The field trip would happen. The van would be ready in the morning.

It was refreshing to be on a road trip, liberated from our tasteful luxury behind the big gate. There was a kind of jovial family vacation atmosphere. Different group members, community people and environmentalists alike, seemed to naturally assume particular roles, probably from their families of origin. There was the organizer, worried about the schedule, about the seating arrangement, about the plan for the day, about the spare tire and the gas tank. There was the carsick one who got the seat in the front, with the best view. There was the one—actually several—who were concerned only with the next meal and the snacks in between. And there was at least one who demanded frequent bathroom stops. Of course, we all whined periodically in unison, "How much longer is it?!" Roberto and I were enjoying our day off.

We stopped on the way into the village to tromp through the mud so that we could get a better look at a four-horned ram that belonged to Gumercindo Salazar. There were photo opportunities, posing with the ram, and when it made a sudden motion toward Bill Waldman of The Nature Conservancy, there were the inevitable jokes about the ram's intentions toward big white men, especially of the environmental persuasion. Clearly, there was a sense of empowerment among the community members. They were on their home turf, and the visiting team was at a big disadvantage, from their logo-emblazoned baseball caps down to their (now) mud-covered Reeboks. The environmentalists were good-natured, trying to hide any discomfort and demonstrate their readiness for adventure.

But the true adventure was not of the outdoor kind. The group arrived at the Ganados del Valle building, which also housed Tierra Wools, in time for lunch. Members had prepared a wonderful spread, including lamb stew, *calabacitas* (squash, corn, and green chiles), a variety of salads, and carrot cake. Tables were set up and we all ate vacation-style, with gusto and no restraint. There were local weavers sitting among us, two or three children, and some surprise visitors. Two women, staff members from the Ford Foundation, had dropped by to visit their grantee Ganados and had naturally been invited by the Tierra Wools hosts to join us for lunch. They took their seats at a small table separate from the group.

Ford funded Ganados and also funded some of the environmental organizations present. And, of course, it funded Western Network as well. I was pleased that the foundation's staff would witness this remarkable coming together of adversaries, and, selfishly, I was pleased that Roberto and I were the facilitators of the process. My encounter with the man from Mora (chapter 2) that opened my eyes to the role of the entremetido had been three years earlier. I was evolving into a more enlightened grantee, understanding the powerful position of being the gatekeeper between the community and the foundation and the resentment it engendered. But I was proud of this particular project, believing that it passed the accountability test because of the participation of the community members in its creation and their acknowledgement that this was something that would benefit them. And the instinct to look good in front of foundation staff runs deep. Like other grantees in the room, I sat up a little taller, smiled a little more broadly, made eye contact a little more often.

After lunch, Maria Varela, who was acting as hostess, thanked us all for making the trip and thanked the community women for the lunch. She asked us to stay seated, get another cup of coffee, and listen to some brief presentations. The community members wanted to educate us in a personal way, she said, about their lives, their values, and their hopes for the future. The speakers ranged in age from twelve to sixty-five. They had obviously rehearsed their speeches, and some were very nervous. There was pressure on them to communicate to this group of powerful outsiders the importance of the economy, the culture, and the lifestyle associated with sheep raising and weaving. One weaver described her involvement in the "sheep-in." Feeling deeply about the struggle for grazing land, she had joined Antonio and Molly at the Humphries, knowing she was risking jail. "And if we have to do this again and that means going to jail . . . I'm going to do it," she concluded.

There was pressure on the audience of outsiders, as well, to be the recipient of such critical messages and to receive them well. When one woman wept while speaking of her concern for her children's future, some of us who are easy criers joined in. Others, particularly some of the men, were clearly uncomfortable. It became clear that this was a key part of the field trip for the community members of our group. We outsiders needed to see exactly what was meant by "attachment to the land and resources," and that meant listening to these voices from Los Ojos. Showing us beautiful pastures, mountain vistas, and a four-horned ram was not what it was about. We had all agreed already that it was spectacular and special land. It was the deeper level of caring, the degree of integration of the land in daily life, that they wanted to be sure we understood. In addition, there was the message that they were the rightful heirs to the stewardship of these lands, that their ancestors had maintained the resources in a healthy state for centuries, and that an environmental movement was not necessary—in fact was a threat—to good stewardship of those resources in the future.

I began to be uneasy. I was feeling vibrations from the environmentalists sitting on either side of me. Here was one grantee presenting her case at the expense of another grantee, in front of the funder. There had been no warning that a foundation would be witness to this event, no agreement that Ford could eavesdrop on this conversation. The environmentalists maintained their composure during the community presentations and throughout the rest of the field trip. But there was serious fallout from this unilateral decision.

Roberto and I, busy congratulating ourselves on having a role in this momentous gathering, had failed to anticipate the problems inherent in the presence of the foundation representatives. Later we agreed that we should have questioned the presence of Ford, talked to Maria and the others, and either set some boundaries on what could be said or asked that the Ford representatives excuse themselves after lunch. Our project with the community members and the environmentalists was about exploring the potential for trust. This had been a serious misstep, and both the facilitators and Ganados were blamed for "setting the enviros up to look bad in front of funders." The van ride back was uneasy. No more family vacation. We passed back through the wrought iron gate and went straight to bed. There was no poker, no beer—or, come to think of it, maybe there was, but I wasn't included.

Roberto and I met early in the morning to try to salvage what we thought was a lost cause. We agreed not to raise the issue of Ford but to deal with it openly if someone in the group raised it. And of course Bill Waldman, the quintessential big white man—with blue eyes, no less—cracked it open. Pulling himself to full sitting height, he blasted Maria, accusing her of creating a "ducks in a shooting gallery" situation. He was angry and hurt and couldn't imagine trusting her again. It was a difficult discussion for the group. Roberto and I hoped to preserve some goodwill and the potential for future talks, but we knew that at any moment it might not be worth it for one side or the other to continue talking, and we had to respect that.

But, as groups sometimes do, this one hung on. Bill remained angry, but he was not going to sink the process over this issue. Roberto and I took responsibility for not acting to protect the group. Maria held her ground, pointing out that she had not planned for the foundation visit and the field trip to coincide. Others spoke with some understanding and insight for both sides. Leaving the incident behind, we asked the group to reflect on what progress, if any, had been made during the past three days. The responses were heartening and a little surprising. People from both camps said that they had made personal connections across the divide and that this had helped diminish their stereotype of the "other." Some admitted that they had experienced a personal insight, one that would change the way they saw things in the future. All agreed that there was an exchange of important knowledge—of all kinds—that would lead to increased accountability and responsibility for both sides. The group also agreed that there is "right on both sides," that these issues are not black-and-white. A corollary insight was that it is crucial to deal with these issues not in a vacuum but as they affect specific communities and specific ecosystems. (The insights were similar to those related in chapter 3 where the tribal and non-tribal county task force members recognized that each situation and each relationship is unique and that blanket rules would not work.)

Finally, and remarkably, many of the participants felt that there was the potential for further work together. The group had struggled, stumbled, and soared, not necessarily in that order. The two sides had said some things to each other that were tough to say and tough to hear. But they had stuck with the process, and that seemed to create a bond, albeit delicate, among them. We laughed about the idea of printing T-shirts—"We Survived the Sol y Sombra Retreat of 1990." When members of such a diverse group can all imagine wearing the same T-shirt, you've got some kind of common ground.

We then asked what obstacles might sink any further progress in relationship building. The list was long. It included the historical backdrop of colonization and the lack of established mechanisms for the two sides to communicate. Without clarity about the problem, the solution—even more elusive—would not be possible. But if the group were to look at the issue of grazing and wildlife compatibility, it could be torpedoed by a war of conflicting data. Group members also worried that if they continued to talk, "mistakes would be made." Everyone knew that was code for "trashing your opponent in front of a foundation." They acknowledged that no one would be able to behave perfectly in a cross-cultural sense, that feelings would be hurt, trust broken. Could they survive these upsets without losing all the progress they had made up to that point?

Considering these potential problems, the group created a list, "Future Conditions for Trust." This guide for behavior for all those who dared to move forward was premised on the assumption that mistakes would be made. The participants wanted to make sure that they all understood these were behaviors to strive for, behaviors that could not be guaranteed:

- Expect to make mistakes; acknowledge them, learn from them, try to forgive them.
- Reveal relevant information, records, and relationships.
- Communicate immediately when there is a problem; don't let it fester.
- Believe what I am saying; don't assume I'm lying.
- Don't set me up.
- Don't bash me in the media.
- Keep the door open.
- Be able to differ with me in a respectful way, to "disengage without malice."

Finally, before our last lunch and our departure from Sol y Sombra, we agreed to take some next steps. The group would meet again. The facilitators would create a written summary of the retreat, to be reviewed and corrected by participants, which would serve as an internal, confidential record of the discussion. Participants would coordinate their media relations whenever possible; as a first step, they developed a joint public statement to characterize the retreat. The following three points were all the outside world knew about the retreat:

- Participants gained a greater understanding of each other's realities.
- Participants agreed to meet again soon and explore solutions.
- Participants agreed that there are "rights" on both sides.

On November 8, 1990, the group reconvened. The members reviewed and corrected my skeletal summary of discussions at the first retreat, which was for their eyes only. They then took a bold step and formed the Pilot Project Working Group, whose purpose was to develop a relationship of trust while working on a substantive project. Members of the group were Maria Varela, Antonio Manzanares, Gumercindo Salazar, Jim Norton (The Wilderness Society), David Henderson (Audubon New Mexico), Bill Waldman (The Nature Conservancy), and George Grossman (the Sierra Club). In addition, Luis Torres, a highly respected community organizer from the Española area, would serve as facilitator, and I was invited to be the note taker.

The Pilot Project Working Group first met on November 29 at Parish Hall in Abiquiu, a compromise location more or less midway between Los Ojos and Santa Fe. The group agreed to pursue the question of whether or not sheep could compatibly graze with wildlife. There were plenty of studies from all over the country and even abroad that could be used to defend one position or the other. But, as they had feared, the two sides could not agree on the validity of any of these studies in the context of northern New Mexico. Rather than beat each other over the head with their preferred research, they decided to gather data together in a joint project. With enough land and enough time, they hoped to demonstrate the compatibility or incompatibility with carefully monitored experiments. The challenge was to find the land. They settled down to draft a funding proposal for $100,000, which they hoped would enable them to buy enough acreage for the research, perhaps using a national organization such as the American Farmland Trust as a vehicle.

To begin the grueling task of writing by committee, the group decided to produce two documents, one from the Los Ojos community and one from the environmentalists, that would describe the problem and suggest goals and objectives for the joint project. The process of writing the proposal was painful as participants struggled to include statements of philosophy and values that reflected both the environmental and the community needs. But if the two sides could not produce a proposal together, how could they possibly co-manage a research project with monitoring protocols, standards, evaluation measures, and more?

In January 1991 the two documents were reviewed by the group in Santa Fe, and I received instructions for merging the two approaches into a single version. Meeting in the late afternoon after a full day of often stressful work, both Ganados and environmental participants struggled to focus and make progress. The folks from Los Ojos had more than a two-hour drive home from Santa Fe, even longer in the winter. (The first meeting had been in Abiquiu, but subsequent ones were in Santa Fe.)

Before that January meeting adjourned at 5 p.m., Bill Waldman excused himself so that he could pick up his four-year-old son at day care. He always picked him up at four o'clock, he said, and nothing was going to stand in the way of his having the joy of driving home together and hearing about his son's day. He was beaming in anticipation. I think he was also feeling that this was a bond everyone had in common, the priority of family; he was sharing that he, like the folks at Los Ojos, valued his children above all else.

It was more than Antonio could bear. He spoke with deep emotion. This was the difference, he explained, between the person who works on the environment for a living, like Bill, and the person like himself who lives the environment. "There is no 'going home after work,'" he said. "I can't just leave this work, because my life and my family's future depend on it. If I fail, we lose everything. I can't afford to fail. You—you can work on another issue, another piece of property, another endangered species. You can even move to another state, find another 'beautiful piece of the planet' and go to work there. I can't do that. I won't do that." He paused. "And by the time I get home from these meetings, my kids are in bed. My son wanted me to read him a story last time, but I had to tell him it was too late and I was too tired. 'It's always too late, and you're always too tired,' he said. It was like a knife in my heart. This work is all about my family, but to do it means that I'm not there for them. It hurts. I wish I could pick up my son every day after school and drive him home. But I'm not there. I'm here. I don't know if it's worth it." It was a powerful message, not lost on the group.

In addition to the chronic internal stress experienced by the group, there was a lightning bolt from the outside that had a severe impact on the fragile alliance. In December 1990, shortly after our retreat, Ray Graham, a wealthy Albuquerque businessman and dedicated environmentalist, filed suit against the Sierra Club Foundation for fraud, misrepresentation, and breach of fiduciary duty. Twenty years earlier, in 1970, Graham had made a \$100,000 donation to the Frontera del Norte Fund of the Sierra Club Foundation with the understanding that the money would support the purchase of a piece of grazing land for low-income, small-scale ranchers in the Tierra Amarilla area. (Specifically, the group that the Sierra Club chose to work with was La Cooperativa Agricola del Pueblo de Tierra Amarilla, a predecessor to Ganados del Valle in the Chama Valley.) This land, Graham had believed, would allow land-based communities to keep land in agriculture but also would serve as a buffer to encroaching second-home development. He wanted to provide a means for the community to support itself on the land in environmentally conscientious ways.

According to a news report published in the New Mexican on May 13, 1992, the Sierra Club Foundation had led Graham to believe that the purchase of land was still being negotiated as late as 1990 and that Ganados del Valle was a leading candidate to participate in the conservation program. Graham became suspicious of the long delay and decided to trace the money. Some research revealed that the money had been transferred from the Santa Fe office of the Sierra Club, which had received it, to the Sierra Club Foundation headquarters in San Francisco. Further detective work uncovered the embarrassing truth. The money had gone to make a down payment on an office building for the foundation in San Francisco. Graham was furious and filed suit for $500,000 to cover the amount of the gift, plus interest, plus damages suffered by the would-be recipient.

Ganados members were unaware of the gift, their role as prospective beneficiary, and their ultimate loss until the story broke in the summer of 1991. By then our small group had produced its draft proposal to fund the purchase of land on which to demonstrate the compatibility of grazing and wildlife protection. Ganados was looking for potential funders when the members learned they had won the lottery and then lost it, without ever knowing it. The environmentalists were deeply embarrassed and feared that the news would adversely affect donations for all environmental efforts. Chagrined before their new allies and partners from Los Ojos, they apologized and did their best to distance themselves from the lawsuit and its fallout.

The Ganados leadership was shocked and furious. Group members had apparently been robbed of what could have been theirs years ago. They might have had grazing land by now and might never have been impelled to break the law and graze their sheep on the Humphries. Even if they had not been the beneficiaries, they were outraged that some other community could have been helped and wasn't. Pressured by community members, and by their attorney, to join in the Graham lawsuit against the Sierra Club Foundation, the Ganados members considered doing so, but at the next project meeting they announced to the environmentalists that they would hold off and not sue. They did not have the funds to join a lawsuit in California, and they wanted to show restraint and not damage the fragile trust that was developing between the community and the environmentalists. The three environmental representatives—David Henderson, Jim Norton, and George Grossman—were grateful and appreciated the courage the Ganados leadership was demonstrating. (Bill Waldman had dropped out earlier, announcing that his board no longer supported his participation.)

Maria, Antonio, and Gumercindo wanted to broaden the discussion to include more community members. They invited those who had participated in the retreat to a picnic in June 1991, and they asked that there be a meeting afterward in which the rest of the community could participate in discussing the joint project and other issues relating to environmental efforts in the area. The picnic was on a perfect day: clear air, blue sky, puffy clouds. The land was beautiful and lush and the host community welcoming and generous. At the meeting, the group discussed the need for the grazing land, the hope for the pilot project, and concerns about the Graham lawsuit. Everyone agreed that the Sierra Club Foundation would be unwise to prolong the litigation and that a trial with publicity would be very damaging to environmental interests. The environmentalists suggested that a settlement could be the answer to everyone's dreams. If the original donation were given to Ganados, the money could be used to purchase the land for the pilot project. But community members emphasized that if they were to receive the funds, they wanted no strings attached. They did not like the idea that their receiving the award would settle any differences with the environmentalists. They wanted the decision about how to use the money—if they got it—to be independent of our process.

At the next meeting, in November 1991, Maria, Antonio, and Gumercindo suggested that it would demonstrate commitment to the fledgling alliance if the environmentalists spoke out in favor of Ganados in the Sierra Club Foundation situation. Understanding that it would mean open criticism of a fellow environmental organization, they asserted that the wrongs done in this case merited public statements from the three. They said they hoped to see a letter to the editor condemning the actions of the Sierra Club Foundation and stating a belief in the capacity of traditional communities to manage resources in environmentally sensitive ways. The three environmentalists said they agreed personally with such a statement but would have to consult with their constituencies, boards, and national offices.

In April 1992, the environmentalists uncomfortably reported that they could not publicly support the Ganados position and condemn the Sierra Club Foundation. The community members asked the environmentalists if they could at least write private letters to the foundation urging settlement of the lawsuit and expressing belief in the rights and capacity of groups such as Ganados. If the environmental allies could not do that, their Ganados partners could see no reason to continue working on a joint project. This was the moment to act like an ally, they said. They were refraining from joining the lawsuit; their partners should offer something in return.

The message from all three environmental organizations was, with deep regret, no. Even a private letter would be disloyal to the environmental community, and that was where their primary allegiance lay. They hoped to continue to work on the joint project to demonstrate grazing and wildlife compatibility. They would go with Ganados to foundations for funding, and they would participate fully in the project if it were funded. If Ganados became the beneficiary of the Graham donation, they said, so much the better.

The group met one more time, in November 1992. Ganados took the proposal off the table, but group members discussed other ways that the environmentalists might help the community. There was talk of marketing Ganados products (weavings and crafts) in the catalogs of the Audubon Society and other organizations. Timber issues were on the front burner for rural communities in the north, and there was hope that this band of enlightened environmentalists might influence their comrades to consider the needs of local, forest-dependent communities in their battle to protect the Mexican spotted owl. But the community members were seriously disappointed by the unwillingness of their allies to defend their position in the Graham suit. For them it was not worth continuing to meet.

Having lost his suit in California, Graham asked Ganados to join him in a suit that involved the Office of the New Mexico Attorney General (responsible for charitable organizations) and the Sierra Club. After long settlement negotiations, a deal was finally struck on the courthouse steps the day before the jury trial was to begin. Ganados received over $900,000, with which the organization purchased a grazing permit in the Carson National Forest, reserving the rest of the money to buy property of its own. Later, Ganados purchased a farm near Los Ojos to be used for demonstration projects.

One year after the last meeting, when it was clear that the Pilot Project Working Group was a thing of the past, Roberto and I reconvened the members for a confidential evaluation session. We were extremely nervous about what people would have to say to one another after the "failure" in alliance building. But we felt it was crucial to understand what had gone right and what had gone wrong, and we were very curious whether any relationships had survived. We issued the invitations and offered stipends to participants to come and tell us all.

First, we learned that connections had been made between individuals on both sides and that those relationships had survived. A community member said she was pleased that an environmentalist, whom she considered her ally, had called her more than once to discuss timber issues and to ask what impact certain actions might have on the community. A network had formed, albeit small and inconsistent, linking some environmentalists and some community members.

Second, it was clear that individuals on both sides understood each other better and appreciated the subtleties and differences among those they had formerly lumped together as the enemy. An environmentalist said that he found himself thinking differently about his positions on local issues and that he had a much more sophisticated view of his own work and rural community needs. A Ganados member confessed jokingly that he had to admit that environmentalists were probably human and didn't have horns after all. The field trip had been an eye-opener and a great educational tool. The efforts of the Pilot Project Working Group to craft language relating to its Problem Statement, Goals, and Objectives had been frustrating but also enlightening. There seemed to be appreciation for our efforts to build bridges between the two adversaries. No one regretted participating.

But the report card on constructive activities was not good. Members of the community felt that the environmentalists had let them down seriously on the Sierra Club Foundation issue. Instead of demonstrating support and a new way of doing business, they said, the environmentalists had behaved like cowards, dumping their new allies at the first bump in the road. Other opportunities had been missed, too, including the environmentalists' lack of foresight about the impact on local people of closing logging roads in national forests. The community had been waiting for their environmental allies to take the initiative, make an offer, lend a hand—something beyond simply crafting document after document or meeting time after time.

The environmentalists pled guilty to many of the accusations and asked for understanding. They were under incredible pressure from their membership, from boards, from leadership that did not share their view that rural communities were potentially important allies. Building a relationship with Ganados, doing work together, was on the agenda, but it inevitably was pushed to the back burner. They regretted this and hoped to find opportunities for mutual benefit in the future.

Finally, the group members drew some conclusions from their experience together. The following is taken from the summary of that evaluation session, as approved by the group:

- If participants are not open to new ideas and ready to change, no amount of meeting and "retreating" will work. Those participants who were affected by the experience, and who changed their viewpoint and behavior to some extent, were predisposed from the beginning to do so. They had the capacity, the curiosity, and the desire to "be in the middle," to see what the other side was all about.

- To bridge cross-cultural differences, everyone—including the mediators—must be sensitive to issues of power. In this case, the environmentalists seemed to have the power of connections, resources, and education. The Hispanic community members derived power from local support and cohesiveness, from political and media savvy, from commitment at a very deep and personal level, and from knowledge about natural resources stemming from lifelong experience with the land. Each mediator also had a certain kind of power based on personality, cultural background, and skills. The challenge is to balance these powers so that communication and learning can happen.

- There is a conflict between wanting to accomplish something concrete together and needing to take time to learn more about one another and develop trust. It is time-consuming, and often uncomfortable, to build a relationship. It can be easier to plunge into a joint project and do something. But if the trust is not there, the project will run into a brick wall, and there will be a new round of disappointment and resentment on both sides.
- There is great power in field trips. The bus trip to Los Ojos during the retreat, the lunch with the community, the presentations, and the visit to see the sheep provided critical education for the environmentalists. The trip also demonstrated the willingness of the outsiders to visit the other team's turf. It was an expression of respect.
- Both sides must understand that there is a fundamental difference in their attachment to the land. For the environmentalists it can be passionate, but the stakes are not what they are for the community. There can be endless arguments about who cares more for the land and the environment, but the quantity of caring is not the point and can't be measured anyway. It is the quality of the caring that is different, and this difference needs to be understood and honored by both sides.

I was fortunate to reminisce with David Henderson many years later, both of us older and maybe wiser. He remembered vividly the confusion and discomfort as he sat down with the Ganados folks for the first time. "We thought we were the good guys, on the crest of the wave of the environmental movement, that if we pounded our fists on the table hard enough we could get what we wanted. We were naive, and they pulled the rug out from under us. We were surprised at the groundswell they generated on behalf of their lifestyle and culture—groundswells were what we were good at," he said with that characteristic laugh. "They had our attention for sure. We couldn't just use our stature, our connections, our education to further our cause. We had to think through these issues more thoroughly than we had historically. We had to really listen."

There were two highlights for him, and interestingly they both related to the land itself. They were the field trip to Los Ojos and hearing the community people speak, and the community picnic on the banks of the Chama River in the summer of 1991. "That was really wonderful," he recalled, his voice warming at the memory. On the downside, he was still troubled by Maria's calling him a racist because she felt he failed to comprehend or appreciate the depth of the community's connection to the land. Not only did the label hurt, but also he felt that she failed to understand the nature and reality of the environmental community, the depth of feeling and commitment to the land and wildlife.

He regretted that the process did not result in a concrete solution for Ganados, perhaps, he speculated, because the decision makers were not present. The leadership of the Sierra Club, for instance, or the American Farmland Trust could have brokered a solution, he guessed. Without that power at the table, the experience became "a seminar of sorts" in which a few advocates on both sides learned a great deal and built some relationships. He valued the experience and credited those relationships with helping him mature as an environmental advocate in New Mexico.

Since our experience with Ganados del Valle, Roberto and I have matured as well. We have facilitated dozens of gatherings designed to bring together land-based community leaders and environmental leaders. We have experienced the same roller-coaster ride time and again—euphoria over a breakthrough, despair over a derailment. We have given up on expecting to make significant changes in the dynamics of the community-environmentalist relationship. We laugh together about how minuscule our influence is and wonder why we persist. But every time, one or more participants will leave enlightened, or at least constructively confused. They will see things differently, let go of a stereotype or a prejudice, maybe even reach out in some way across that cultural divide. That is enough to keep us going. In fact, that is a lot.

CHAPTER FIVE

Finding Common Ground

It was 1993, and the nuclear waste negotiator was a desperate man. I am not making up this title. The Office of the Nuclear Waste Negotiator was a short-lived independent agency of the US federal government responsible for the placement and storage of nuclear waste from 1987 to 1995. Its head was responsible for finding some place—any place—willing to store spent fuel rods from the country's 111 nuclear power plants. This high-level radioactive waste was being kept at each plant in unsafe conditions, and both the public and the administration insisted on a safe, secure facility ASAP. David Leroy, the nuclear waste negotiator, sent letters to every state, tribe, and county soliciting a host for a temporary MRS (monitored retrievable storage) facility for the waste. Permanent underground storage was being negotiated at Yucca Mountain, Nevada, but even under the most optimistic scenario that site would not be ready for forty years. What was urgently needed was a place to house the spent fuel rods in the interim, a nice, well-monitored aboveground facility.

With only two people per square mile, San Juan County, in southeastern Utah, is classified as "remote" by the US Census Bureau, one step below "rural" on the population density scale. One-third of the population lives below the poverty level, and although the county has experienced oil, gas, and uranium booms in recent decades, any lasting benefit has been erased by the devastating busts. The county has cultural and scenic richness and has received attention from the film industry and from recreationists, most recently rafters and mountain bikers. Over half the county's population is Native American—Navajo and Ute Mountain Ute—and the majority of the rest are Anglo, many from Mormon families who settled the area a hundred or more years ago. There is also an active environmentalist crowd and a scattering of Hispanic families. One-quarter of the land base in the county is Native American, the vast majority being the Navajo Nation, which occupies the southeastern corner of the county (and state).

Exhausted by the boom-bust cycle, residents in 1993 were ready for a more stable economic base to address a variety of problems—an inadequate school system, communities under increasing economic and social stress, and a high unemployment rate. Scanning the horizon for possibilities, the county commission stumbled upon an intriguing possibility. Mr. Leroy was offering significant benefits for any area chosen to house the MRS facility, as well as jobs during construction and operation. To some, it looked like a match made in heaven—a federal agency desperate to find a site for the storage of high-level radioactive waste and a county desperate for economic stimulus.

If the county responded to the invitation with an expression of interest, it would receive $100,000 for Phase I, an initial screening to determine the feasibility of the site. There would be no strings attached and no obligation to continue with the process. This in itself looked like a good deal to the two Anglo county commissioners, who outvoted the Navajo commissioner to accept Mr. Leroy's offer. Phase I included a cursory exploration of locations and a polling of public opinion. If the results of this first phase indicated that the population was seriously interested in studying the feasibility of the facility, the county could apply for Phase II funding—a much bigger amount—and begin the study process in earnest.

The nuclear waste negotiator had advised the county commission to hire an outside consultant to design and conduct the public involvement in order to ensure a credible, unbiased process. Western Network was asked to submit a proposal, and although it was a public involvement and survey job rather than conflict resolution, we decided that our skills could extend to cover this scope of work. (We eventually adopted "public involvement" as a legitimate offering, having found that what might begin as public involvement could evolve, for better or worse, into more traditional conflict resolution roles. See chapter 6.)

I began work in the spring of 1993, determined to reach the public, in all its variety, ask the following questions, and deliver the answers in a report to the commissioners:

- Do you want the county commission to explore the feasibility of siting an MRS facility somewhere in the county?
- What concerns do you have about the MRS facility, and how can your questions be answered in a way that is credible and understandable?

I knew this was going to be a highly contentious proposition. Not only was radioactive waste a hot topic, but for some in this corner of the Wild West, consorting with the federal government was an even hotter one. I met with the three commissioners and proposed a public involvement process that I thought would accommodate the county's diversity of culture and language, its sparse, spread-out population, and its level of poverty. They agreed to a series of community meetings, school visits, a newsletter, a toll-free telephone comment line, and radio advertisements. And, maybe, I added, we could form a citizens' advisory committee to advise the commissioners about moving forward.

I spent the next six months commuting back and forth from Santa Fe to this beautiful corner of Utah, holding public meetings in community centers, elementary school gyms, and local cafés. I was interviewed by radio stations, spoke to the Lions Club, and put out a newsletter with a tear-out survey. It was a challenge to offer enough information about radioactivity and spent fuel rods to make people knowledgeable without either panicking them or boring them to death. Eager to land a candidate site, Mr. Leroy's office provided stacks of brochures about nuclear power plants, "Dear Neighbor" letters to the citizens of San Juan County, and even videos explaining the MRS facility siting process. I found that the best approach was to try to explain it all as best I could in my own non-technical words and then offer materials.

Tackling Navajo country was a challenge. In order to reach the Navajo residents, I needed to visit each of the five chapter houses—seats of local tribal government—in the county. The monthly chapter meeting is an important event to the rural Navajo, worth traveling a long distance for. It offers you a chance to hear from your Navajo Nation Council representative about goings-on in Window Rock, Arizona, capital of the Navajo Nation. You can catch up with friends, pick up commodity foods, hear the latest from the Navajo Area Indian Health Service worker, maybe even sign up for a computer class or get your dog vaccinated for rabies. I knew it would be easy for me to get on the agenda and be guaranteed a full house. And, having lived on the Navajo reservation for almost eight years, I was always eager to return, even on this somber subject.

But Navajo tribal government is hierarchical, and I knew I should pay my respects to the nation's headquarters in Window Rock before going to visit the chapter houses. Early in the process, I had written letters to the president and the head of the Navajo Environmental Protection Commission asking for a meeting to discuss San Juan County's MRS facility siting proposal, and after no response, I had followed up with phone calls and faxes. Four months had gone by, and I was getting desperate. I knew that others in my place might "check the box" saying that they had tried to reach the Indian population but had received no response and so were moving on. I was determined to have the Navajo voice included in my final report, and so I decided it was time to go straight to the grass roots.

I explained my predicament to the Navajo county commissioner, Mark Maryboy, hoping he would give me permission to address the chapters. He was too savvy to make that mistake and end up crosswise with Window Rock, but he did give me the name of an interpreter who could go with me—if I decided to go ahead. We both knew I would and exchanged smiles over our parting handshake.

First on my schedule was Navajo Mountain Chapter House, of the five the deepest into Navajo country and farthest from the pavement. I began early in the morning from Kayenta, Arizona, where I had spent the night in a motel near Monument Valley. It was a calm Saturday in July, hot and dry. The sky was cloudless, and the blue was even more vivid against the red rocks that appeared as I neared the turnoff to Navajo Mountain. These last twenty miles were dirt washboard, and as I bounced along I felt oddly at home in this remote corner of Utah. Although I had never been to this chapter house in my time on the reservation, I anticipated seeing familiar faces, feeling that soft and gentle handshake, smelling that smokiness from the hogan fire on people's clothes. I was nostalgic for a home that I knew wasn't really mine but that could raise those emotions in me just the same.

As I approached the end of the long road and saw the building in the distance, there was a catch in my throat. I knew what lay a couple of hills beyond the chapter house—Lake Powell and what is now Rainbow Bridge National Monument. This is the community most affected by the flooding that resulted from the construction of Glen Canyon Dam on the Colorado River. The dam was built between 1955 and 1965 to provide water and electricity for millions of people downstream, none of them on the Navajo reservation, by the way. The ancestors and artifacts of the Navajo Mountain community are buried under a thousand feet of water, where tourists now water-ski.

The site of the chapter house is spectacular, perched among red rock formations, smoothed by eons of erosion and sandblasting from the brutal spring winds. I pulled up next to the building, looking for shade but finding none. The ride had jiggled and bruised both me and the dozens of apricots I had brought from our ancient and abundant tree in Santa Fe. I knew the fruit would really be appreciated at Navajo Mountain, and I smiled at the thought that some of the pits might be saved and planted in the spring. Maybe someday there would be a little shade from a couple of apricot trees.

I was early and had plenty of time to set out my boxes of apricots in a prominent place and the boxes of materials in a less prominent place. Navajos trickled in, helped themselves to coffee, and seemingly after a lot of consideration chose a folding chair from the hundred or so arranged for the meeting. My interpreter arrived with an aunt and uncle who lived nearby and joined me up front. Although we had gone over the presentation and he had figured out how to translate some of the tougher concepts, such as "half-life" and "spent fuel rods," he seemed nervous. In a way, this would be harder for him than for me. I was the outsider; he was a Navajo working for the outsider.

When the chapter president moved to the rough wooden podium, the crowd settled and the meeting began. After preliminaries, I was asked to introduce myself. My Navajo language skills had never gone beyond discussing animals, children, food, and vehicles, but I said a few words in

Navajo, which brought laughter and piqued the interest of the crowd. I explained my role and where I was from and offered my homegrown apricots. And then, through interpretation, I gave the message of the nuclear waste negotiator to the chapter members, just as I had for other assembled citizens of San Juan County.

The reaction was unanimous and negative. My interpreter was struggling, not just with the language but also with being there, and I was more and more uncomfortable in my supposedly neutral role. We heard one after another heartfelt speech. An elderly Navajo woman began to cry. "You already have done enough to us. Please leave us alone." The "you" hit home. Of course it wasn't me, but I was the emissary not just of the nuclear waste negotiator but of the Anglo world in general. The uranium boom in the 1970s had ripped up sections of precious Navajo land and ruined the health of many Navajo miners. Some had died, others were very sick, and even family members were beginning to show symptoms. The elderly woman was speaking of these tragedies, but underlying her words were memories of other abuses visited on Navajos in earlier decades. There was the sheep slaughter by the Bureau of Indian Affairs in the 1930s, the damming of the Colorado River that flooded the sacred canyon, the "rape" of Black Mesa by coal companies, the mistreatment of Indian children in the boarding schools, and undoubtedly other, less public offenses as well.

Once it was very clear that the waste was not welcome in Navajo country, I raised the question of where it might be stored safely. "Maybe they can shoot it into space, since the government seems to like to spend money doing things like that," suggested a young man. There was a little laughter, but an older man cautioned against sending it to the moon, for spiritual reasons. After dozens of people had spoken, the chapter president declared it was time to move to the next agenda item. I packed up my materials—the same full box I had arrived with—and quietly left. A boy was eating an apricot outside. His grandma, sitting next to him, smiled at me and said "Ahéhee'." Thank you.

At Navajo Mountain, and at my later chapter house visits to Red Mesa, Mexican Water, Aneth, and Teec Nos Pos, I heard people struggling to hang on to values and beliefs belonging to a culture that is under attack from powerful forces such as consumerism, digital technology, drugs and alcohol, and environmental contamination. I saw people clinging to a way of life based on the natural resources around them—the dryland plots of corn and squash, the precious water, the sheep and goats, tinted red from the dust kicked up as they grazed. The idea of siting an MRS facility near Navajo country was the last straw. If the rest of San Juan County was divided on the question, Navajo country certainly was not.

I also visited schools on the reservation. I wondered what this kind of proposal would look like to young Navajos. Would they be swayed by the potential for jobs? Would they be afraid? Would they have heard parents and grandparents—like the woman at Navajo Mountain—crying over the thought of bringing the waste to Navajo country? An eighth grader at the junior high school in Aneth was one of several who listened to me with remarkable attention and were very thoughtful about the problem. "It has to go somewhere," he said, "and wherever that is, they should just look at it, keep their eye on it all the time, never stop watching it, so nothing happens to it." His classmate, a tall, long-haired girl in a Simpsons T-shirt doubted the promises in the video that the spent fuel rods were safe to live near. She said, "If the president of the United States lived next to the MRS, then I would feel safe living next to it, too."

And of course, right after my last chapter house presentation, at the end of August, I received a call from Window Rock. Tribal staff wanted to discuss the MRS facility siting proposal in San Juan County. Of course, I said I would be delighted to come and visit with them, but in contrast with most trips into Navajo country, in which my eagerness grew with each mile, this one filled me with apprehension. I feared that my decision to go to the grass roots without first consulting with Window Rock might not sit well with the bureaucracy.

I pulled into the parking lot. The Window Rock itself was up to the left, so beautiful against the deep blue sky. I paused for a few deep breaths, got out of the car, and entered the stucco tribal building. I found the office of the vice president and introduced myself to the receptionist. She asked me to wait, and after a few hushed phone calls she escorted me to a conference room with a huge table and chairs to match.

In a few minutes two women and two men, young and Navajo, came in with briefcases. They looked very serious in their casual business wear. The women wore pantsuits, one gray, the other black, with white blouses and silver bracelets. The men had on khaki pants, pastel button-down shirts, and ties. They were all well-groomed, well educated, and, one hoped, well paid, the new bureaucratic elite of the Navajo Nation.

I had a special feeling for these earnest staffers. They were younger than me, and I could imagine them growing up on the reservation in Chinle or Tuba City, going to college, and coming back to work for what was now called the Navajo Nation. In a sense, I knew where they came from, and I valued that place; it was part of me, too. But that was not relevant here. I was a contractor to San Juan County, one of many local governments bordering the Navajo Nation, most of which had reputations for discrimination and hostility toward Navajo people and their government.

We exchanged names and shook hands. The heavyset young man with short hair was a staffer for the vice president. The others were with the Navajo Environmental Protection Commission. I offered my traditional Navajo-style dead fish handshake, and they offered an Anglo-style firm grip. I said a couple of words of Navajo as a greeting and received a weak smile from one of the women. They sat down, opened their briefcases and manila folders, and fiddled with pens and yellow pads, the preliminaries to a meeting. The staffer to the vice president was reading from his open folder, pushing his horn-rimmed glasses up on his nose occasionally. It was hot, and I heard one woman tell the other that the air-conditioning was broken again. The vice president's staffer loosened his tie as he flipped the page he was reading. With a little shifting, I could see it was the letter I had written to the president months earlier requesting an appointment to discuss my planned activities. Once I had begun the chapter visits, the voice of Window Rock had seemed less important to me, but at this moment it suddenly seemed critical. I was already intimidated by these silent, serious bureaucrats.

The vice president's staffer looked up, the others ceased their fiddling, and he asked me to explain what my intentions were with the five chapter houses. I was eager for them to know that I was no ordinary Anglo, and so I began with a brief introduction. I had lived in Chinle, I had a deep appreciation for Navajo culture, and it meant a lot to me to extend my professional life into Navajo land. I had really enjoyed my meetings at the chapters, I added.

The taller of the young women, the one who hadn't smiled at my Navajo words, interrupted. "You have already been to the chapters?"

I realized that they didn't know I had bypassed them. "Yes. I talked to Mark Maryboy, and I had an interpreter—"

"You had an interpreter? Where was he from?"

"He was from Aneth. He was very good. We went over some of the technical terms in advance. I know how hard it is to translate complex words—"

"You should have come here first, before you went to the chapters. Protocols are very important, extremely important." She was glaring at me. I could feel myself blushing. I struggled to maintain some dignity and defend myself at the same time. I wanted to tell her that protocols go both ways and that my cultural protocol says that you answer letters in a timely manner, not five months later, that I knew all about tribal sovereignty and the importance of respecting tribal government, and that I was a nice person and didn't deserve this berating. I could say none of that. I needed to endure and get out of Window Rock in one piece.

"I wanted to do that. That was my plan. I wrote to the president's office and to your office, twice, and made several phone calls . . ." Here I paused ever so slightly to give an opening for an explanation or even an apology, but neither came. "I was under a deadline, and—"

I was interrupted midsentence by the smaller woman, who apparently felt I needed to have the question repeated. "Why did you go to the chapters without clearance from Window Rock? You shouldn't be out there contacting Navajo people with your own interpreter." Window Rock was responsible for the health and welfare of the Navajo people, she emphasized. How did they know that I was trustworthy? How did they know the interpreter wasn't corrupt and lying to people?

I replied that I understood the sovereignty of the Navajo Nation and that I wanted to be respectful in working in Navajo country, but the time line for the project necessitated my moving forward. Leaving Navajo residents out of the process would have been clearly unfair to that important segment of the county. I hoped they could understand that I was dealing with these Navajos as citizens of San Juan County.

She responded, and was backed up by others, saying I should have been accompanied by central office representatives to monitor how the presentations were made and ensure that the right message was delivered. I apologized for disrespecting the protocol and explained that my job was to gather all the information and opinions that I could from citizens in the county and to be sure that those citizens were treated equally and were equally free to speak to me, with the promise of confidentiality. Taking a deep breath, I said that being chaperoned by Window Rock at the chapter meetings would not have been appropriate. Jaws set around the table; eyes narrowed. The county commissioners, I said, had asked the same thing, but I refused. Citizens have a right to participate directly in a democratic process such as this without the influence or interference of their government. I knew I was on thin ice, but I wanted them to see there was a principle here.

I received another lecture and made another apology, and then, blessedly, that portion of the agenda seemed to be over. The staffers went on to ask about the chapters' responses to the proposed MRS facility. I described almost unanimous opposition to further study of the proposal, which seemed to mollify them. We talked a few more minutes about the MRS facility siting project, and they explained their concerns about the health risks of transporting the waste through Navajo country and storing the waste in San Juan County. I took notes and assured them that I would include their points in the report to the county commission. And then they were looking at their watches and their Day-Timers and I knew it was time to go.

I thanked them for their time and said that I hoped they understood the choice I had made and that I was sorry for any disrespect that I might have shown. There were some mumbled good-byes and another round of handshakes, and I followed them down the hall, turning left and out the door as they turned right and into the inner sanctum of tribal government.

Although our parting was civil, I imagined they were thinking, "What do we have to protect ourselves from now—facilitators? Who are these people with their principles? Don't they understand how critical it is to protect our land, our resources, and our culture and that there is a hierarchy in place to ensure that protection?" And, for me, I was wistful for my earlier life in Chinle, where I had been known and trusted, where I had belonged, at least for a while. I had fought for Navajo voting rights and economic justice, and there had been some small victories. And now, years later, I imagined that I was defending the individual rights of the Navajo residents of San Juan County. But it wasn't that simple.

I did a lot of thinking as I drove back to Santa Fe. I was a mass of emotions—embarrassed to have been accused of insensitivity and disrespect, angry at what felt like their arrogance, and confused about what I should have done. Was I being too rigid in insisting on some kind of direct citizen participation based on my own culture's belief in the ideal system of government? Was I undermining in some subtle way the authority of the Navajo tribal government, eroding its hold on its citizens and, eventually, its culture and resources? History is loaded with examples of abuse of all kinds visited on Navajo communities by outsiders. To these earnest young tribal bureaucrats, I may have looked like another suspicious, meddling outsider. In the end, I told myself that my job was to ensure that every citizen, from every culture, could participate in a process such as this one, to have a direct say in actions that will affect them. Ideally, I would have visited the tribal environmental agency before going to the chapter houses and negotiated their role in a respectful way. But "ideal" is rarely available.

I had begun my public outreach efforts among the non-Indian county residents in April and continued through July, finding a very different set of challenges from those in Navajo country. No matter what day of the week, what time of day or night, what kind of refreshments I promised, where I placed announcements, or what those announcements said, I was unable to attract more than a handful of people. People were apathetic or tired or both. "The government will do what it wants anyway." "I work all day, running the kids everywhere. I'm just too tired at the end of the day." And there was a lot of competition for precious evening hours. "There's softball Monday, church group Tuesday, Lions Club every other Wednesday; Thursday I cook for my mother; Friday, well, I gotta have a night off!" Okay, I thought to myself, I will go where they are going anyway and see if I can catch their attention. And that is how I came to sit in front of the post offices in Moab, Bluff, and Blanding.

I set myself up with a card table, three folding chairs, my MRS facility materials, and my trusty flip chart. On the sidewalk, as close to the door as I could get without impeding traffic, I lured people into conversation as they came to pick up mail. From among this steady stream of people some stopped to chat, learn a little something, or voice an opinion. I wrote on the flip chart a few words from each conversation relating to the pros and cons of the MRS facility siting proposal, or I handed over the marker and let people write their own words on the big paper. Late in the day, the front of the post office would be wallpapered with these sheets, a chronology of words and ideas collected during the day. People would gather in front of the papers reading the opinions of their community, nodding, fuming, or chuckling over their neighbors' comments. Groups formed and continued talking about the proposed MRS facility among themselves. I was pleased with the "go to where they are" strategy, and I have used it many times since.

The strategy also introduced me to some memorable characters. In Moab, as I was baking on the sidewalk one June afternoon, a clean-shaven, red-faced rancher stopped at my table, curious about this lady from somewhere else and what she had to say for herself. I said what I had to say for myself and explained about the MRS facility proposal. He took time to educate me a little.

"The uranium came out of the ground here in Utah," he said. "It's everywhere, all around here. Those fuel rods might as well come back here to stay." He smiled, and stuck his thumbs in his belt so that his hands framed his belt buckle. "Little lady"—he was building up to a finale—"do you know what this is?" He tilted back on his heels slightly so that I could see under the overhang of his belly. He nodded at the large rock on his belt buckle. "That is uranium ore! Yep, right there. Wear it all the time. I'm sure as hell not afraid of a whadda-ya-call-it facility to store the stuff. Put it in my backyard if you want."

Near the end of the day in Blanding, an older man, a retired miner, pulled up a folding chair to sit with me awhile. He had lived there all his life, built a house, and raised three children. And could I guess what he used as foundation material for his house? The answer was uranium tailings. No problem; made a fine building material. We went on chatting, about life in Blanding, about changes he'd seen, about children and grandchildren. Well, he said, he guessed he had been unlucky. One daughter died several years ago, in her twenties—some kind of tumor. His other daughter lived in Florida, and doctors were trying to figure out why she was so tired all the time and losing so much weight. His son was okay, though. That was good. "Yep, those tailings make a real good foundation material," he added.

The results of all this public involvement were a surprise to me. After I collated all the comments from the meetings, surveys, calls to the toll-free number, and radio call-in shows, it was clear that the county was divided, but the equal number of pros and cons was remarkable. Almost all commenters had already made up their minds and felt passionately about the subject. Forty-five percent opposed the facility, felt it would be an environmental disaster that would bring little if any economic benefit, and believed that anyone favoring the study was ignorant, if not evil. Another 45 percent favored the facility, saw it as an answer to economic prayers, and felt that opponents were hysterical, weak, and trying to ruin everything that might bring some progress to the area. Both those opposed and those in favor felt that more study about the proposed MRS facility was not a good idea. Opponents said it might lend credibility to the idea and there was already plenty of information to show that it would be a disaster. Proponents said that the government had already wasted too much money on studies and that there would be plenty of safeguards and protection at the facility.

It seemed that by raising the subject and inviting public participation, the county commission had succeeded in dividing citizens against one another—in a county already seriously divided along cultural, economic, and values lines. The passionate 90 percent overwhelmed and silenced the 10 percent who wanted to learn more. The idea of proceeding with a democratic, participatory study process was becoming less and less likely.

The commissioners had wanted a clear answer, or, rather, two of them wanted a clear yes answer, and the other, the Navajo, wanted a clear no. But all I would be able to recommend was a referendum on the subject, and that was what they had hoped to avoid, at least until after they received the generous Phase II funding.

One option we had discussed at our first meeting had been a citizens' advisory committee, a representative group of citizens to offer guidance to commissioners on how to proceed with the feasibility study process. Telling me to "get it over with as soon as possible," they gave consent for me to hold one meeting only. I knew that the committee would be polarized on the MRS facility issue, but I hoped committee members might rally around a different topic. After all, the sheep-raising community and the environmentalists in the previous chapter had been willing to meet as long as the hot topic was off the table. Maybe, like them, the divided population in San Juan County would find some common ground if they left the MRS facility question at home.

Diverse as the population was—Anglo, Native American, Hispanic—and different as its interests were—ranching, mining, recreation, business, environmental protection, education—I had heard some assumptions that I hoped could form the basis for conversation about a better future:

- A devotion to the land based on history, culture, economics, religion, or its sheer beauty
- The need for an economic boost
- The poor quality of education and the emigration of youth from the county
- The deep divides that drove county residents apart

Committee representation was chosen by the interest groups and communities themselves, with a little oversight from me. I was looking for diversity in gender, culture, age, and economic background along with a willingness to listen—and, I hoped, a dose of imagination.

The goal, I said in my invitation letter, was to identify problems facing the county and talk about solutions, and the response was gratifying. The fifteen-member advisory committee included an outfitter and river guide, a geologist, a miner, a rancher, two high school students, two small-business owners, a school principal, a Bureau of Land Management employee, two tribal government leaders, a homesteader, an environmentalist, and a homemaker. The one-day meeting would be held at the elementary school library in Bluff, the geographic center of the county, and participants would receive a stipend and lunch.

It was an icy November day, and the group straggled in, stamping feet and unwrapping scarves and heading for the doughnuts and coffee. Everyone was good-natured and apparently in the mood for some kind of adventure, the first step of which was getting seated around the low tables on pint-sized chairs. The high school basketball star looked particularly comical. The introductions were revealing. We discovered that the senior citizen director from Navajo Mountain had had the longest drive, and we gave him a round of applause. We also found that we had a great-grandmother among us, that one of us had been born in Florida, that one of us had two PhDs, that one of us was "small-business woman of the year in Utah," and that three of us spoke Navajo, one spoke Ute, two spoke Spanish, and one was a retired rodeo champion.

I welcomed them all as official advisory committee members, commissioned to identify problems facing the county, consider the roots of those problems, and suggest solutions. I held little hope for any agreement, given the cultural and economic diversity of the group. How could a devout environmentalist, a uranium-mill worker, a part-time farmer, and a high school junior agree on what's good for the county? How could a traditional Navajo, a Mormon elder, a Hispanic Catholic, and a Protestant from Connecticut reach common conclusions about the future of their region? How could a rancher and a federal land manager, or an aging hippie and a retired miner, even sit at the same (tiny) table together? I hoped only for some increased understanding among the group members.

But as they talked about what they valued about where they lived, common themes emerged—the same ones I had heard in prior months. Both natives and newcomers loved the landscape—the canyons, cliffs, red-and-gold rock formations, green ribbons of cottonwoods along the washes. They liked the quiet; they treasured the clear air; they valued their remoteness. Some talked about the value of the area's history and its close association with the land and its people. The Mormons spoke with pride of the Hole in the Rock, through which a Mormon caravan had passed, almost miraculously, in the 1880s. The Native Americans spoke of mythology and religion and the significance to their cultures of certain land features and locations. Ranchers and farmers spoke of the tradition of working the land and ensuring its sustainability. Miners spoke of the role of mining in developing the area and added with pride that San Juan County contributed important natural resources to the rest of the country. There was a sense that an awareness of history—both in this world and in the spiritual world—must be preserved by those in the present, for those in the future, on behalf of those in the past.

During the discussion, I saw people listen to each other seriously. Defenses were lowered, postures relaxed, expressions softened, and when someone spoke, there was emotion—not of trying to beat up the other side but of trying to make the other person really understand. Three big problems rose to the top immediately: economy, education, and divisiveness. Group members described what desirable economic development would look like for the county. They listed stability and well-paid jobs for local people as criteria for new development, adding that the enterprise should not endanger human health or the environment and should be as aesthetically pleasing as possible. They measured certain potential projects, including a state penitentiary and a microchip factory, against their list. Highest ranking were small home industries, the film industry, tourism, and telecommunications or the high-tech industry. I held my breath waiting for the MRS facility to come up, but the group knew it didn't need to go there.

Education was another big concern. There was not enough money; there was the potential for corruption at the school board level; good teachers left; good students never came back. Education and economy were tied together, they said. Until there was a well-educated workforce, good economic development would not settle in the county. And until there was a strong, vital economy, there would be no quality education system.

Finally, as the day continued and we finished our box lunches, group members began to talk about what seemed saddest and most confounding to them. They called it the "splits." There are splits, or divisions, everywhere in the county, they said, cultural, religious, economic, philosophical. Indians versus non-Indians. Mormons versus non-Mormons. Old-timers versus newcomers. Rich versus poor or poor versus poorer. Environmentalists versus business and industry. They told stories of these hostilities being played out in school yards, at sports events, at community gatherings, on election day, at Walmart, Pizza Hut, or Taco Bell. Some told of being victimized by the divisions. Some confessed to perpetuating the divisions. There were historical roots and reasons for the splits, they admitted, but it was time for healing.

At the end of the day, the committee members all agreed on a one-page resolution, which they asked me to deliver to the county commission. The resolution began: "The Citizens' Advisory Committee requests that the Commissioners enter into a dialogue with the county residents, so that decision makers and constituents can better understand each other's needs and move toward a common vision for a healthier county." The committee members went on to describe what they meant by a healthier county:

- The economy is stable, with well-paying, safe jobs.
- Education is of the highest quality and equally available to all the county's children.
- The county's cultural, political, and economic diversity is an enrichment rather than a source of divisiveness.

The resolution also asked for leadership in beginning a healing process that would bring San Juan County residents together on the basis of their common feelings for the land and resources of their unique region.

The one-meeting-only citizens' advisory committee adjourned at 4 p.m. The members unfolded themselves from the elementary school chairs and creaked into standing positions. There was an ease in the group, a quiet satisfaction. It hadn't been that hard to come together, talk and listen, learn and understand. Maybe it could happen again. The committee members all agreed to continue to serve in this role if the commissioners accepted their invitation. They said tentative good-byes, not sure if this was the beginning of a relationship or the end.

It turned out to be the end, at least in that context. The county commission received my final report, which included the citizens' advisory committee's resolution. A newly elected governor vetoed any further study of the MRS facility proposal by the county. The two Anglo commissioners continued to push for the right of the county to make its own decisions in spite of the veto. Opponents formed a coalition and, backed by the governor, pushed the county to give up any thought of further study. Another split had been created. As far as I know, the county commission never reconvened the advisory committee or responded to its offer to enter into a dialogue about the county's future.

But for me, the highlight of this story was that day in Bluff when a diverse group of people gathered in an elementary school library to model a new beginning, a way of healing the "splits."

And one particular moment I remember fondly. The slowest-talking, slowest-moving committee member was the outfitter and river guide, a hermit and eccentric of sorts. In his fifties, he was known to be a radical environmentalist and was rumored to have been the inspiration for a character in an Edward Abbey novel. Perhaps his slowness was the reason he was the last one out the door, helping me load my coolers in the car. I thanked him and added that I really appreciated his taking the time and effort to be part of this gathering. It was not necessarily a compatible group for him, I said, and I realized that he was somewhat isolated as an avowed environmentalist. He laughed, running his fingers through his unruly hair. "Oh, no, this was much better than spending the day with a bunch of environmentalists! These people were damned interesting—good people—worthwhile for sure. Hell, I almost had fun!" We chuckled and said good-bye, got in our cars, and pulled out of the parking lot, headed in opposite directions.

CHAPTER SIX

The Army Corps Takes Orders

Colonel Michael DeBow, district engineer for the Albuquerque District, US Army Corps of Engineers, stands in full uniform in front of an angry Hispanic crowd in the Abiquiu elementary school gym. It is fall 1992, and he has just arrived for a two-year rotation as head of the Corps in this region. He has convened this public meeting in an effort to reach out to the members of the community and inform them of the agency's activities in the area. Specifically, he wants the local ranchers and irrigators to understand the problems at Abiquiu Reservoir. It is the responsibility of the Corps, he says, to provide a safe environment for recreational users, but the reservoir is crowded, and there are increasing conflicts between these users of the public waters of the United States and local residents. Can the community help the federal government protect these swimmers, boaters, and jet-skiers?

The crowd is not in a helping mood. They accuse the colonel of a long list of crimes—construction of the dam in the first place, current Corps policy and actions, insensitivity to community needs, and finally just being an outsider, in every respect. Whether he knows it or not, he is the recipient of stored-up venom against every abuse ever visited by a government agency on this traditional rural community in the past 300 years. The colonel is flanked by his uniformed staff, but there is no one who can interpret into Spanish for him, and that is the last straw. "Who do you think you are?" and "Where do you think you are?" they shout. The colonel has encountered the deep Hispanic roots of northern New Mexico. By the end of the meeting, he is seriously battered and disturbed by what has happened. Why are these people of the Rio Chama Valley so angry? How is he going to make the improvements he sees necessary at the reservoir in the face of this kind of hostility?

The Rio Chama begins in the mountains of northern New Mexico and flows through beautiful high-plateau country into the Rio Grande north of Santa Fe. The stretch through Abiquiu is Georgia O'Keeffe country: dramatic red-and-pink cliffs, deep blue skies, and rolling hills dotted with sage, piñon, and juniper. This natural beauty surrounds several small traditional ranching and farming communities whose Hispanic roots go back as many as eight or more generations, back to the colonization of the region by the conquistadores. These communities use the river to support ranching and to irrigate rich bottomland through an intricate system of acequias, hand-dug and hand-maintained ditches.

In recent decades, the Chama has been used for rafting and sportfishing and as a conduit for a large quantity of water imported from the San Juan River, a tributary of the Colorado River. The San Juan's water is diverted from one side of the Continental Divide to the other through a tunnel that dumps the water into the Chama for its trip to the reservoir, where it is stored. When Albuquerque, owner of most of the imported San Juan–Chama water (200,000 acre-feet), gets thirsty, the water is released and continues its journey, flowing down the Chama, joining the Rio Grande, and eventually being diverted into the city's treatment plant. All this is possible thanks—or, in many local minds, no thanks—to Abiquiu Dam, built for flood control and water storage for a variety of downstream customers.

When the dam was authorized in 1955, the National Environmental Policy Act (NEPA) did not exist. NEPA requires that any federal agency, when contemplating an action that might impact the environment, neighboring communities, or other interests, must analyze those potential impacts, develop a range of alternative actions (including the "no action" alternative), and make its decision in an open and accountable public process. The environmental impact statement (EIS) is the compilation of all the studies and analysis. Since NEPA's passage in 1972, advocates of all kinds—from environmentalists to traditional communities to business interests—have depended on this process to ensure that they have a say in how these decisions are made. It is hard to imagine (although some industries and some bureaucrats might welcome it) a world without the EIS. Had NEPA existed in 1955, communities neighboring Abiquiu Reservoir would have had an opportunity to see the Corps' plans, make comments, and perhaps negotiate a more favorable deal than they received.

The reservoir created by the dam flooded over 6,000 acres of prime grazing land, for which landowners were compensated $7.00 per acre. Although the landowners retained ownership of the land surrounding the reservoir, in 1960 the Corps had acquired a flowage easement (Public Land Order 2159) for that ribbon of land. This gave the Corps the right to raise and lower the level of water in the reservoir for safe and efficient dam operation. The result was either banks that were underwater or exposed mud.

Anger grew with each year that passed. Residents considered the dam just one more abuse in a long line of actions that damaged the community's economic and cultural fabric. Whether it was the New Mexico Department of Transportation, the New Mexico Department of Game and Fish, the federal Bureau of Land Management, the US Forest Service, the Sierra Club, the rich developers, crooked lawyers, or just plain "outsiders," in the eyes of these communities the Corps was the latest and worst abuser.

But as resentment grew, so did recreational activity on the reservoir. In this arid state, the small reservoir quickly became known as Abiquiu Lake, attracting thousands of boaters and other recreational users every year from all over the region. By the 1980s, the Corps staff—now recreation managers as well as dam operators—had become concerned about public safety. With only one entry and exit point on the lake for boats, there was serious congestion at some times of the year and some times of the day. Limited access to the lake also meant that boaters were trespassing on private property if they went ashore to hike, fish, or picnic or if an emergency forced them to land. Windsurfers were blown onto grazing land, either intimidating or being intimidated by cattle. Ranchers were less than hospitable—on at least one occasion armed and ready to fire—when hikers or picnickers strayed onto their land. There were reports of dangerous conditions caused by weather, irresponsible or ignorant boaters, visitors, animals, and landowners, in various combinations.

In 1992, the Corps concluded that to protect and serve recreationists, it needed to expand facilities around the reservoir, adding boat ramps and picnic and camping facilities and designating safe swimming areas. Public Law 100-522, signed in 1988, gave the Corps the authority to "acquire lands" on which it held easements, if necessary to ensure proper recreational access. The time had come, thought the colonel, and he proposed to acquire 6,044 acres of grazing land and 66 acres of residential land, currently part of the flowage easements and described in the Corps announcement as "an uneconomic remnant." This proposed federal action triggered the NEPA process and necessitated an announcement in the Federal Register: the US Army Corps of Engineers was intending to acquire the land and to undertake a full environmental assessment and EIS.

Colonel DeBow hoped to be able to purchase shoreline property and easements from various landowners necessary to access the new recreational development. But everyone knew that the Corps had the authority to condemn the land if necessary, land currently owned by the same Hispanic ranchers who had run the colonel out of the community center a year earlier. Not wanting to further inflame the community by using the word "condemn," the colonel insisted on using the term "forcibly acquire." But this, of course, only added to the local anger.

Most vocal were Hispanic ranching families who traced their landownership back more than 250 years and their ally, Ghost Ranch, a Presbyterian retreat and conference center. The facility drew hundreds of visitors each year to take courses, contemplate the beauty of the area, and find some inner and outer peace. Ghost Ranch supported the senior rights and standing of its neighboring residents in the area, believing that the interests of the agrarian users most closely mirrored their own interests of peace and solitude. Another ally was the New Mexico Department of Agriculture, which testified to the importance of the livestock industry in the economy of the state and the region.

New neighbors had joined these interests at the lake. Since, and because of, the construction of the dam, small subdivisions and second homes had sprung up on the northeastern shore. The Abiquiu Lake Homeowners' Association was vocal about its needs for access to the lake, freedom to use the lake, and protection from trespassers. As was the case with other recreational users, association members' opinions about development and management of the resource varied, depending on their preferred activity. Jet-skiers and "no wake in the lake" folks may not have seen eye to eye, but they and everyone else were unanimous in their opposition to the Corps' proposal to acquire more land. The wounds from the loss of land some thirty years earlier to create the reservoir were still very fresh, and now that there were processes such as NEPA, which mandated consultation with all the interests, the community hoped that such loss would never happen again.

But the future of the reservoir included other players as well, distant geographically from Abiquiu and with their own interests and rights. Clearly, the lake was an economic boon for some, and real estate agents from nearby Española and Santa Fe were eager for improvements that would increase the value of property in the area. Environmental groups and the New Mexico Department of Game and Fish were concerned that additional facilities at the lake would increase traffic and activity, with impacts to the natural beauty and wildlife, including bald eagle nests upstream.

There were also those below the dam who could be affected by recreation decisions for the reservoir. Downstream irrigators, organized as the Rio de Chama Acequias Association, were worried about the quality of water in the reservoir and the timing, size, and number of releases from the dam. These releases could destroy the fragile structures of the acequias if they were too large or too sudden. Home owners downstream had the same concerns about homes built in the floodplain, and this dispute revived old fears about the safety of the dam itself and the geologic fault that might lie beneath it. Hearing their upstream neighbors mutter about dynamite as a solution did not ease their fears.

And finally, whether from New Mexico or New Jersey, the public user—the client so often cited by the Corps—had a claim to the reservoir. Fishing groups (fly and bait), boaters (powered and non-powered), rafters, birders, and hikers all had their particular angles on the expansion of facilities.

Having been badly burned at the community meeting the previous year, when he appeared without an interpreter, the colonel had experienced firsthand the hostility of Abiquiu residents toward the government in general and the Corps in particular. He realized that imposing a solution to his safety problems would only further enrage the community. He hoped to use the scoping process required by NEPA to negotiate a solution with the community that would meet the Corps' need for recreational safety and the community's need for a rural way of life. Scoping calls for informing the public about the proposed federal action and taking into consideration—and here, of course, there is great debate about how far the agency must go—any problems identified by the public. The results of scoping help define the socioeconomic, cultural, and environmental studies that will make up the EIS and form the basis for the final decision. To design and facilitate a credible public involvement process that would satisfy the requirements of NEPA, and would enable him to appear in public without being shouted at, the colonel hired us at Western Network. We had experience, and we had staff who were native northern New Mexicans and who spoke Spanish.

The first hurdle was to help the Corps let go of the process. Here was an agency founded on military principles and steeped in military culture. Decisions were hierarchical; control came from above. Although the colonel and his staff knew that they needed help, it was counter to their instincts to give up control. During our talks with them about how the public meetings should be organized and managed, they clung to a certain rigid format. Staff favored formal, technical language in their informational materials rather than the clear, abbreviated approach we recommended. They begged for time limits on speakers; we knew that would just lead to audience frustration. They wanted ground rules that would require those attending a public meeting to "leave their emotions at the door." That was insulting, we said, and impossible to enforce anyway. Then how, asked Colonel DeBow, could we guarantee that things would not get out of control? I assured him that we had the skills to handle the most ornery crowd. What was important was that the community members believed their views were valid and were heard. That was the colonel's job: to listen and learn.

After delicate negotiations, the colonel agreed to follow our recommendations. There would be four public meetings, each preceded by an open house period during which Corps staff could help citizens look at maps and other materials, learn about the problems at the lake, and talk about solutions. These open house events would take place in four different communities—Los Alamos to the south, Española to the east, Abiquiu at the lake, and Coyote to the west. To be sure of good attendance, we suggested some preliminary work—talking with people, distributing flyers, and the like.

This was a frightening thought to the Corps staff. Why would we want to "arouse" people, get them excited ahead of time? Wouldn't it be better to just quietly advertise the meeting, see who came, hope for the best (a few well-behaved people), and go home? We reminded them that it was very important to be open and all-inclusive and that if people suspected the Corps was being sneaky or less than honest, it would be curtains. We assured the colonel that what we were suggesting would meet his needs; he needed to trust us. All he and his staff had to do was relax and listen.

As a final preparation, we held a public meeting "dress rehearsal" at the Corps conference room in Albuquerque. Colonel DeBow, in his forties, was bald, wore black-rimmed glasses, and had a pleasant face and a physical bearing marked by good posture, efficiency of movement, and a quiet confidence. He was someone who took his leadership role very seriously. He seemed, in fact, to take everything very seriously. He smiled rarely, not because he was unhappy or angry but because he was doing his job, being responsible, thinking through the best strategy, whether he was building a bridge or anticipating a public meeting. It would be hard to imagine the colonel knocking back beers at a bar, and if he did he certainly would not be slouching and probably not telling jokes, either.

He was in uniform for the rehearsal, looking very military and manly. Attempting to inject a little humor, I asked if he could take off his uniform for the public meetings—and wear something less formal, I quickly added. His staff snickered at the thought of the colonel taking it all off at a public meeting, but he didn't crack. He had given in to me on so many points, but here he stood up a little straighter and informed me that it was a matter of law that he be in uniform. He would allow his staff, however, to dress engineer-casual for the meetings.

We went through the welcoming remarks and the presentations on the NEPA process, the problems at the lake, the proposed solutions. And then we facilitators role-played angry, disruptive citizens while the Corps staff practiced responding. The colonel continued to have doubts, questioning us over and over about the process. At the last moment before exploding, I had a revelation. The Corps' hierarchical system depends on someone giving orders and someone taking orders, and it is important that everyone knows who gives and who takes. "Colonel," I said carefully, "you have a highly structured organization, which runs smoothly because you have experts giving orders. Well, in this case, you hired us to be your experts on public involvement, right?" I got a nod in answer. "So, all you need to do is take orders from us. We are the experts on this one." I wasn't as sure as I sounded, but I guessed that was part of how the hierarchy worked, too. The colonel obediently took orders from us after that. And, in fact, it was more than just a matter of taking orders. Some of the principles of sound public processes seemed to be sinking in.

By the time the scoping meetings began, the colonel was committed to the kind of open, equitable process that we had been preaching. If by chance the meetings were to result in a clear and workable solution to the problems at the lake, and if that solution were legal, he agreed to adopt it as his remedy. The colonel had actually initiated a negotiation process with the community—by hiring facilitators, by giving them control of the process, and by entering the meetings with an open mind. He was turning into the ideal client.

The four public meetings were held within an eight-day period between March 27 and April 3, 1993. Over 400 attended at least one of the meetings—a remarkable turnout for such a rural area. The colonel was true to his promise. He and six staff members attended all four open houses (2–6 p.m.) followed by public meetings, two of which lasted beyond 11 p.m. They followed our orders very well. At the public meetings, the colonel made brief welcoming remarks and then joined his staff, who were scattered throughout the audience. They spoke only when spoken to, listened intently, and learned a great deal.

The emphasis was on the public. This was their chance to comment on the proposed land acquisition and a lot more. We knew there would be an avalanche of anger flowing toward the Corps, and we made room for it, keeping track of the points on flip chart paper. By the end of each evening, the walls were covered and the colonel's yellow pad was full of his own notes. Although the four public meetings were set in different locations on different nights to allow citizens to choose the most convenient time and place, the majority of the audience traveled to at least two, and in many cases to all four, meetings. Presentations were carefully crafted to build on each other from one meeting to the next. Certain groups—the Ghost Ranch and the traditional ranching families—allied and developed mutually supportive positions and choreographed their presentations. And the colonel's opening remarks evolved as well, building in a responsive way on what he had heard at the previous meeting. The result was a dialogue and a negotiation, rather than simply a series of meetings, between the colonel and the heart of the community.

The community message was strong. Recreation brought damage and grief to local residents. The community would not tolerate condemnation of one more acre; enough had already been lost to the dam. There were threats of congressional intervention to prevent condemnation, of lawsuits, of public awareness campaigns, and of use of the media, and always there was the real possibility of this community taking matters into its own hands. But the colonel heard more than the threats; he heard the reasons.

As with the Los Ojos community (chapter 4), many of these families had been on the land for over 200 years. For them the land, water, forests, and wildlife were not just resources; they were part of the social, cultural, and even religious fabric of the community. More than one speaker cried over the loss of beautiful areas already flooded by the dam. A woman at the Española meeting railed against the Corps. "The lakeshore looks like a dirty bathtub ring," she said, "with rotting trees, floating stumps, and mud. Soon the trees and stumps will float away, just like our culture and way of life." She closed to thunderous applause. Those downstream of the dam described the devastation caused by the sudden releases—huge volumes of water rushing through fragile irrigation systems and wiping out handmade headgates and diversion channels, structures that had served the irrigators for generations.

No one had asked the community members how they felt about the dam in the first place or, for that matter, about any of the other abuses visited upon them by agencies, by lawyers, by developers, by armies of exploiters, and more. All of these actions, they said, had hurt the physical, economic, and emotional life of the community. And this was the last straw. The Corps was going to take more land, cut up ranch land with more roads, develop more recreation, and usher in even more invaders to spoil the rural life. "It feels like being a prairie dog," said one man at the Abiquiu meeting, "drowned and run out of your hole, over and over again." The scoping meetings were an opportunity to tell the government just how it felt to have suffered abuses in the past and to have no control over your future.

Constructive ideas were raised at the meetings as well. Could the Corps do what it needed to do with less land? Could it negotiate with willing sellers? Could it limit recreation at the lake? Could it increase the size of the existing boat ramp rather than develop new ones? Could it bring in additional enforcement to control drunk boating and vandalism? Could parts of the lake be designated no-wake? Could private landowners develop recreation facilities themselves? What controls could, or should, there be on that development? Could better, more informative educational materials be given to recreationists showing them the private landholdings and explaining the unique nature of the area?

At the second meeting, the colonel opened by saying that he had listened carefully the night before and had heard passion and commitment to the land and water resources. He also had heard deep resentment at the Corps' suggested land acquisition. He was offering an alternative way of resolving the problem—creation of an Abiquiu Lake advisory council, a forum in which the Corps and community could work on a solution together.

The community was interested but skeptical. Who would sit on this council? Would it really have any power? Was this just a diversionary tactic? Most important, said a community leader, if the colonel was serious about working with the community, then he should end the EIS process, because as long as that threat of condemnation exists, "it feels like you are holding a gun to our heads, and that is no way to work together." The colonel answered that he would make his decision about the EIS after the final meeting. On April 2, between the second and third meetings, New Mexico senator Pete Domenici issued a press release. He applauded Colonel DeBow's proposed citizens' advisory council, and he asked the Corps to halt its plans to acquire additional land for improvements at the lake until the recreational needs could be thoroughly studied.

At the third meeting, the colonel repeated his offer of working together. He had been moved by hearing the depth of feeling for family and for place. He talked about his own childhood on a farm in the Midwest and how he felt about that particular piece of land and community. He was making an effort to connect with these people who were trying so hard to reach him.

Among the pleas to stop the EIS process, there was acknowledgment that the colonel seemed to be really listening, that he seemed to be a decent person. There were questions about his tour of duty. How much longer would he be colonel in this district? In a few months, he said, his two years would be up, and he would be assigned elsewhere. There was an audible sound of disappointment. He would be sorry to leave this special place, he said.

At the fourth and last meeting the testimony continued, and the colonel continued taking notes on his yellow pad until the last comment. And then he stood up to make his final remarks that would signify the close of the public involvement process. He walked to the podium, adjusted his glasses, and began to read slowly from his yellow pad, as if he were hearing his own words for the first time, as if he wasn't quite sure what was going to come next. He had appreciated the willingness of people to come to these meetings, he said, and to open up in the way that they had. He understood the depth of their attachment to the land and the depth of their anger and mistrust of the Corps. "Trust takes a long time to build, but it can be destroyed in a minute," he said. He wanted to begin that slow rebuilding of trust with the community. He knew it would be difficult, and he had thought a lot about how to do it during these meetings. The audience was motionless.

He went on. There were different ways he could approach the problem of safety at the lake, and he wanted to work with the community to find solutions. But he knew that trust was crucial to a successful partnership, and he knew that in order to be worthy of trust he would have to halt the EIS process, "remove that gun from the head," he said, using the community's phrase. And there, in the Coyote Elementary gym, he read a notice that would be published the next week in the Federal Register withdrawing the EIS process. The audience exploded. They stood and cheered their new hero. "Who knows?" said a Coyote rancher. "Maybe there will be a song someday about you—a *corrido*—you'll be like a folk-hero colonel." An Abiquiu resident stood, presented a copy of *The Milagro Beanfield War* to Colonel DeBow, and said he would buy him a steak dinner. There were more than a few teary eyes, including those of the facilitators. And, come to think of it, the colonel was smiling a quiet smile.

The next period was a honeymoon for everyone. The colonel had become a folk hero; the community had been empowered; facilitation had played a key role. The agency, the community, and we at Western Network were all setting out together on uncharted seas, creating a partnership between the Army Corps of Engineers and the Abiquiu community. With no more EIS scoping process, the Corps amended our contract to include consultation with the community to form the Abiquiu Lake Advisory Council and facilitation of meetings between the Corps and the council once it was formed.

Implementing the colonel's idea and moving from an EIS process to a Corps-community partnership was hard work. Divisions began to appear in both the Corps team and the community alliance. Not everyone within the Corps was supportive of the colonel's change of heart and direction. Although the chain of command was clear, with the colonel in charge, many staff members were entrenched not only physically in the Albuquerque or Abiquiu office but also mentally in an attitude that opposed negotiation. They had the power that comes with longevity in a position and a place, and they were able to subvert the colonel's vision by simply carrying on with business as usual.

Like the Corps team, the unified community front began to crack. With the Corps no longer the common enemy, different segments of the community fell back to their old positions. The ranchers pulled back from the developers at the lake. The downstream irrigators pressed for a dam release schedule that would hurt lakeshore landowners and white-water rafters upstream. The jet-ski crowd turned on the no-wake crowd. The Ghost Ranch, still an ally of the old ranching families, suggested that its visitors' experience might be improved without cows and their pies.

But the colonel was determined. On April 22, 1993, he announced in the Federal Register the formation of the council "to assist the Corps in evaluating alternatives generated during scoping for an EIS addressing proposed land acquisition to assure proper recreational access [and] to advise the Corps on future issues regarding Abiquiu Lake." The Corps made it clear that the community was responsible for formation of the council. The staff wanted to avoid jumping through the hoops of the Federal Advisory Committee Act (FACA), which would apply if this council were created by a federal agency (see chapter 8 for more on FACA). As long as the council was a community entity, the colonel would be happy to attend its meetings and talk about mutual problems. The Corps had no requirements for the council but suggested that the more representative it was, the more credible it would be. If a select few tried to stack the group, the Corps would have to consult with others to ensure broad representation on issues. The council, the colonel suggested, should include someone who could speak for the outside recreational user—that public which the Corps is compelled to serve and protect.

For four months the community struggled with the mission, goals, and structure of the council. One of the first actions of the group was to demonstrate unity (at least in name) against the Corps by changing the name of the council from the Abiquiu Lake Advisory Council (the colonel's designation) to the Abiquiu Reservoir Advisory Council (ARAC), which group members felt more accurately reflected the man-made nature of the problem.

We Western Network facilitators ran the ARAC meetings, mediating among the members, drafting mission statement after mission statement, and eventually finding consensus on a council structure. The council would have nine seats—three ranching families, three subdivision representatives, one Ghost Ranch representative, one downstream irrigator, and one public recreational user. Members agreed that they would operate by consensus and that consensus meant unanimity. This eased some of the anxiety about numbers of seats on the council and the potential for one side outvoting the other. (See chapter 8 for more on consensus.)

Filling the "public recreational user" seat on the council was a dilemma. Each council faction tried unsuccessfully to install "one of theirs" in the seat, but eventually, after months of stalemate, a boater from Española seemed acceptable and joined the council. His lack of history with the process, however, and a difficult personality, were problematic. He opposed most of the council's recommendations concerning boating safety and limitations on recreation, and he fought the consensus rule and eventually made it unworkable by vetoing almost everything. He wanted to deal directly with the Corps, favoring much of what the agency had proposed originally in the way of development of the lake, and he was the proud dissenter on almost every issue. The ARAC circumvented him to some degree by working at the subcommittee level with the Corps on specific issues, but his presence added to the frustration level at each meeting.

By the time the council was finally formed, in September 1993, Colonel DeBow, the folk hero, had finished his two-year tour of duty, and there was great anxiety about the intentions of his replacement. Colonel DeBow had told the community members that he was instructing the new colonel to watch all sixteen-plus hours of videotapes of the four public meetings so that he would understand the situation and the commitments made by the Corps. The new colonel may not have been pleased with that legacy, or with his first homework assignment, but he promised to obey the order. He said he felt sure that there would be enough willing sellers to piece together the needed access, but, he added, he could not give up the right to condemn that land as a last resort, sending the community into another tailspin.

The council never gave up its fear that the Corps would condemn land around the reservoir. It seemed to be almost a comfort to council members to return to that passionate issue that had once unified them. First on the agenda for several months was a report on lobbying efforts to change the congressional act that permitted land condemnation at the reservoir, and the New Mexico delegation was scrutinized for portents, good or bad. Rather than focusing on negotiating solutions at the reservoir for safer recreation, council members were always hoping that a political solution could manipulate the situation in their favor.

Another problem for the council was the complexity of the issues. There were the City of Albuquerque's legal rights at the reservoir; there were the technicalities of stream flow management, including the interbasin transfer from the San Juan River and the impact of any action on the whole system; there were wildlife and endangered species issues; there were the matters of economics and of calculating benefits to the area from existing and future development. And not the least of the challenges facing the council was to understand the many ongoing government processes in the region, including the Corps' recreation master plan revision, the county land use plan, US Forest Service and Bureau of Land Management resource management plans, and water rights adjudications, to name a few. It was hard for ARAC members to keep up with all these issues and processes, given the demands of their daily lives and the distractions created by squabbles, mistrust, and fear.

Finally, there was a problem in the ever-shifting role of Western Network. Although we did nothing illegal, I believe we evolved too easily, becoming too many things to too many people. First we were the designers, consultants, and facilitators of a public involvement process for the Corps. Then we became community organizers and mediators, helping citizens strategize to form a council in order to negotiate their interests with the Corps. From there we moved into facilitating ARAC meetings, trying to play a neutral role with both the community members and the Corps. In straddling the line between the interests, moving to one side and then the other, I believe we lost, rather than gained, credibility.

During formation of the council, some community members suspected that we had a Corps agenda, since we were still being paid by the Corps and had been working for the Corps in the EIS process. There was also some discomfort with the concept of consensus that we pushed and with our facilitation of the council meetings. If this was a community council, said the council members, they should be in charge. Unable to let go, we changed our role yet again, becoming scribes to the council chair, who ran the meetings.

And to be sure that we caused distress for both sides equitably, we raised the suspicion among Corps staff that we were biased in favor of the community because of our central role in the formation of the ARAC. The new colonel, however, did not share this view and encouraged us to continue.

Looking back, I find it clear that the whole scoping process and its surprise transformation into community empowerment was a heady, fairy-tale experience for us that we were not willing to give up. It had been intoxicating and we were still high, unwilling to believe that anyone else might better serve the process, unwilling to admit that our usefulness had expired. The relationship between the Corps and the ARAC did survive and produced some useful agreements, including revision of the ten-year recreation master plan for the reservoir. The council subcommittees met regularly with Corps staff to deal with specific issues such as boat safety and education of recreationists. The results included a new brochure for users of the lake, signage forbidding swimming in certain areas, designation of a no-wake area, and increased law enforcement. The new master plan was adopted in 1996.

Most significantly, the Corps did not condemn—did not even "forcibly acquire"—land around the lake. The agency scaled down its original concept for development and was able to buy from willing sellers the small pieces of land it needed. To date, Congress has not changed the authorizing language for the reservoir that gives the Corps condemnation powers, and I'm sure that community members still shudder when they think about that possibility.

For me, this is a story about the power of listening deeply and responding as a human being, from the heart. The colonel was courageous to put himself in the hands of facilitators, civilians at that, and follow their orders. He was a model of thoughtful decision making and wise leadership. Looking back, I value Colonel DeBow most for being able to acknowledge that he was wrong and to change his mind. That quality makes him an exception in my experience, in a career filled with one self-righteous protagonist after another.

And to be completely honest, I have to say that this story also provides a lesson for the facilitator. The process, the setting, the players can be very seductive. It is easy to fool yourself into believing you are indispensable, that the group could not possibly take the next step without you. It's hard to let them grow up and fly away.

CHAPTER SEVEN

A Rugged Road

Matt Magoffin drove his white 1977 Chevy truck down a dusty road on his 22,000-acre ranch in the southeastern corner of Arizona. The spring had been brutally dry, and checking on water sources around the ranch was critical this time of year. He was especially worried that a certain earthen stock tank might have dried up. A red-faced Scotch-Irishman in his early forties, Matt had brown hair and blue eyes that were often on the verge of smiling . . . but not today. Before he opened the truck door he saw the remains of the water he was looking for—a mud puddle, turning to potato-chip curls of dried clay around the edges. But there was worse news to come. He lowered himself from the cab and walked to the tank site. As he approached he could see that the little frogs were running out of water quickly, barely able to cover their backs. Across the tank he watched a coyote reach in and slide a frog down his throat. Herons, too, had joined the feast, and Matt knew that snakes and other predators were sure to finish them off. They needed enough water to hide themselves or they were goners.

When a rancher finds an endangered species on his land, it is bad news. In 1995 and in the middle of a serious drought, Matt Magoffin was that unlucky rancher. The tiny frog with a big name, the Chiricahua leopard frog, was struggling to survive in the remnants of an earthen stock tank. Matt knew that the US Fish and Wildlife Service was concerned about the sharp decrease in this little fellow's numbers and that the agency was considering adding it to its threatened species list. Making a living by running cattle in the Chihuahuan Desert was hard enough without having to deal with the restrictions that would come with this designation.

"Shoot, shovel, and shut up" was the answer for many ranchers in Matt's position. If you found anything on your property that might be of interest to the environmental community or the government, you should get rid of it as quickly as possible. Pretend it never happened, and hope it wouldn't happen again. It was an understandable instinct, particularly in areas, such as the Chihuahuan Desert, where ranchers felt under siege—from Mother Nature, from environmental activists, and from local, state, and federal land management agencies.

So what did Matt Magoffin do when he realized he had a vulnerable species on his property? For three months, until the next rain, he hauled 1,000 gallons of water a week for the frogs. Why would a desperate rancher, whose own way of life was very much in question, devote himself to the survival of a tiny frog? It is a fascinating story and one that gives me hope for a future in which those with a stake in western open spaces can work together.

The Chihuahuan Desert bioregion crosses the Mexican border as well as the Arizona state line into the Boot Heel region of New Mexico. It is beautiful, rugged country that includes three mountain ranges—the Peloncillos ("bald ones" in Spanish) and the Animas in New Mexico (whose ridge is the Continental Divide) and the Chiricahuas in Arizona. The mountains, at least to a visitor, are bare and intimidating, a jumble of huge crags as high as 8,000 feet jutting into the relentless blue sky. But these mountains shelter a network of canyons, streams, arroyos, and valleys, home to a great variety of vegetation and wildlife, including over 300 bird species and over 85 kinds of amphibians and reptiles. The Boot Heel serves as a corridor for species migrating between the tropical regions of Mexico and the northern temperate climate. It is famous among birdwatchers for the numbers and varieties of hummingbirds and famous among hunters for its deer, antelope, and bighorn sheep. There have even been jaguar sightings. But unfortunately, the wildlife corridor also serves criminal traffickers, and today drug runners pose a serious threat to residents of the area.

The region is also home to a handful—only a hundred or so—of ranching families like the Magoffins who have run cattle over large tracts for three or four generations. Ranching here is hard, on people and on cattle. The vegetation is sparse at best—desert scrub and tobosa grasslands—and the ratio of land to cattle is expressed in number of acres per cow, not number of cows per acre. One cow needs forty to fifty acres to survive. Ranches are tens of thousands of acres. One might ask why anyone would even try to raise cattle in this inhospitable place. The answer any rancher will give you is this is home, this is where we are, this is what we do—past, present, and future. Like other land-based communities—the acequias (chapter 2), the sheepherders (chapter 4), and the ranchers in the previous chapter—life in the old days was easier in many ways. The Boot Heel ranchers struggle to hang on in the face of a diminishing resource, increasing regulations, and political and social trends that often seem a threat to their survival.

My introduction to ranching in the Chihuahuan Desert came at a land and water conference in Utah in 1994, a year before Matt had the encounter with the frog. I was there to learn more about grazing issues and to make connections with agency, environmental, and ranching folks. Our experience at Western Network with the Ganados del Valle sheep ranchers and the environmentalists had moved us to look for other ways to bridge those traditional divides and find that elusive common ground. I was beginning to despair after a morning of academic presentations when a big cowboy from the Boot Heel with a lot of miles on him stood up to speak. It was Bill Miller. Over six feet tall and heavyset, he was dressed that day in cowboy formal wear—polished boots, pressed jeans, blindingly white starched shirt, bolo tie with turquoise, and a mouse-colored felt cowboy hat. He was in his sixties, with gray hair peeking out from under the hat. He took his place at the front of the room, adjusted his hat, and grabbed the sides of the podium as if he were about to throw a bull to the ground. He had an engaging way, self-effacing, down-to-earth, and clearly confident that he had something to offer the conference goers, no matter what their allegiances. He had a story to tell, he said, about getting desperate enough to try something different.

Bill had been sitting late one summer afternoon on Warner and Wendy Glenn's big front porch, a frequent gathering spot for far-flung neighbors. They were talking about ranching and the forces—natural, political, social, economic—that seemed to be conspiring against them. It seemed that no one understood the challenges they faced, and no one valued their way of life or their contribution to the economy, the culture, and the environment. They were also worried because it seemed that every generation inherited poorer and poorer grazing land. It was painful to admit that the land was deteriorating under their stewardship—as the environmentalists were quick to point out, Bill added.

Part of the problem, Bill said, was the fire suppression policy of the federal and state land management agencies in this region, called the Malpai Borderlands. Just recently the Bureau of Land Management had barged in and put out a brush fire that was heading toward the ranchland. Without regular burns—natural or prescribed—the grasslands necessary to maintain the ranchers' way of life were being taken over by woody species such as mesquite, cholla cactus, and other desert scrubs. The government didn't understand and didn't seem to respect the ranchers' knowledge or needs.

But, Bill explained, there were worse threats to their way of life. With support from foundations and armed with masses of research, environmentalists were on the rampage. And they had laws behind them, namely the Endangered Species Act, which in his eyes they seemed to take personal responsibility for enforcing. The Chiricahua leopard frog, for instance, was a candidate for the threatened species list, and from there, Bill and his colleagues knew, it was a short hop to the endangered list. They knew it was only a matter of time before the frog—or some other species of interest—would be spotted on one of their ranches. The rancher could find himself host to this unwanted guest, accountable for its health and survival and saddled with restrictions from yet another federal agency, the US Fish and Wildlife Service. They could see the handwriting on the wall, and here Bill raised his voice for emphasis. They—he and his neighbors—were the next endangered species, and if they didn't do something quick, they would be the next to go extinct.

Calling themselves the Malpai Borderlands Group, this small group of ranchers chose a creative strategy to address these threats. The laws, the money, and the popular sentiment were too powerful for them to take on the opposition. They needed to prove, Bill said, that the ranching way of life and a healthy landscape could go hand in hand. They needed to join their adversaries—the agencies, the scientists, the environmentalists—and form some kind of alliance dedicated to maintaining and improving the great open spaces (federal, state, and private) of southeastern Arizona and southwestern New Mexico. They hoped there was some common ground; at least, Bill pointed out, the ranchers and the environmentalists shared some common enemies—encroaching subdivisions that were eating up the open spaces, degraded land that needed fire and reseeding, and drought. At this point in his narrative, he pulled out a copy of the 1994 Malpai Borderlands Group newsletter and read from it. "Although we couldn't influence the rains, we could work together to change the other problems. We could enlist the help of the very people who misunderstood us."

They decided to take an unprecedented step. They would actually talk to The Nature Conservancy. They had been befriended by a conservancy staffer in Virginia, John Cook, who had taken a special liking to the land and culture of the area and suggested that there might be some overlapping interests. Perhaps there were others like him at the local office in Tucson. But approaching The Nature Conservancy was a very risky step to take. "No one jumped up to volunteer," Bill said with a laugh. "I drew the short straw." He told of getting ready in his best pressed ranch wear to go meet the enemy, settling the hat on his head, and hoisting himself into his pickup. He got more and more nervous, he said, as he neared Tucson. He had the address, and once he found the street he drove along slowly, looking for the number. He couldn't believe he was actually going to enter enemy territory, where dwelt those who made it clear they wanted every cow off every piece of federal land (and private, if they could manage it).

He saw it: The Nature Conservancy sign over the storefront office. There was a parking place right in front, but he just couldn't stop. He drove past and went around a few blocks to make another approach and, he hoped, land this time. But once again he drove on by. He repeated these drive-bys and finally gave up and parked down the street a couple of blocks. He walked to the phone booth on the corner, dialed the number of the environmental office, and asked the staff person to please meet him at the coffee shop down the street. Bill didn't reveal the details of the meeting, but it was obviously a first step in building an alliance between the Boot Heel ranchers and a leading environmental organization.

He laughed at himself when he told the story, but it was a powerful illustration of the deep animosity between the two sides and the risk he had taken in reaching out. Bill's engaging presentation was the hit of the conference. He was offering a vision for a collaborative future in which bold leadership could come together to do the right thing for the environment and for people. Of course, the impetus for the Malpai ranchers was one of self-interest and preservation, but who's to say they can't go hand in hand? What he and his neighbors were doing was revolutionary, and I could feel the whole audience wanting to jump aboard.

From this low-key introduction, the Malpai Borderlands Group quickly grew to be the toast of the western land management world. Funders and partners were eager to support this refreshing new approach to land stewardship, in which ranchers and environmentalists work with the land management agencies to improve the health of the ecosystem and maintain a ranching way of life. The size, location, and ownership mix of the land within the group's boundaries offered opportunities to make significant changes. Today the Malpai Borderlands Group encompasses nearly a million acres in an area shaped like a pyramid, with the base stretching from Douglas, Arizona, east along the Mexican border to Antelope Wells, New Mexico, and the apex near Animas, New Mexico. Landownership is 60 percent private, 20 percent state trust, and 20 percent federal.

The group's first joint project, a comprehensive fire plan for the area, fielded an impressive number of partners: environmentalists, scientists, the US Forest Service and Natural Resources Conservation Service, the Bureau of Land Management, and the Arizona State Land Department and New Mexico State Land Office. A next big step was establishing a "grass bank." Thanks to The Nature Conservancy's purchase of the 300,000-acre Gray Ranch, the Malpai ranchers had access to alternative grazing land when their own lands were suffering drought or other hardship and needed a rest. In exchange, each participating rancher agreed to a conservation easement on his land, guaranteeing that it would not be subdivided and would be monitored for signs of deteriorating health. Today over half the Malpai lands are under conservation easements, eligible for technical assistance from agencies and universities to restore land, slow runoff, contain sediment, reduce erosion, and increase vegetation.

Matt Magoffin had joined the Malpai Borderlands Group, and when the Chiricahua leopard frog turned up on his ranch in 1995, he was ready to put the new strategy into action. Instead of "shoot, shovel, and shut up," Matt declared that what was good for the cattle was good for the threatened species, and vice versa. The Malpai Borderlands Group and its partner The Nature Conservancy raised money to help install a well to pump water for the frog. Of course, the ranchers' primary motive was probably to avoid the regulations that would come down on them if the frog were declared threatened or endangered. But this is a perfect case of congruent interests, in which the frog, the ecosystem, and the ranching community were all victors. They even took on another species, the thimble-sized Cochise pincushion cactus. The group's 1995 newsletter announced a new joint project with a research botanist to monitor the health of this endangered plant species. The Malpai Borderlands Group was on a roll, partners in the conservation of this precious landscape and its inhabitants.

I became a Malpai Borderlands Group groupie, following members through their newsletter and crossing paths with them at workshops and conferences. They were smart and courageous, I thought, and I was hoping for some role as facilitator or mediator. The opportunity that arose in 1996 was not the one I hoped for, but because it took me to the Boot Heel and because it involved Bill Miller I agreed to mediate a dispute between neighbors.

Bob and Katie Scholes, avid bird-watchers recently retired from Virginia, had moved two years earlier onto a landlocked property next to that of Bill and Carrol Miller. Their only access was a seven-mile dirt road that wound through the Millers' ranch. The Scholeses arrived with great enthusiasm for their new home, having no idea that their love of birds would brand them as environmentalists, still a highly derogatory label in those days in the Boot Heel. The ranchers felt the sting of the environmental push to eradicate grazing on public lands, and they fumed at bumper stickers like "No More in '94," which they took personally. Both in their seventies, the Scholeses had walked innocently and ignorantly into the lion's den or, more accurately, across the lion's savanna.

Bill Miller, from one of the oldest ranching families in the area, was the lion of this savanna. He and Carrol had a classic log-and-stone ranch house on the southern edge of their 8,000-acre ranch, facing a great expanse of grazing land with the Peloncillos rising up to the right. The first mile of the access road was in Arizona and the rest was in New Mexico, meaning that different state laws applied to easements.

In Miller's eyes, the Scholeses were out to get him. He suspected that they might even be a front for some big organization with an agenda to eradicate cattle from the earth. They were university types—Bob a professor, Katie a public health nurse—and that made them elitist, with their fancy education. And perhaps worst of all in his eyes, they were from back east and therefore had no understanding of, or sympathy for, the ranching culture of the Southwest. Why hadn't they stayed in Virginia, where they belonged? After all, the Millers had stayed put in the Boot Heel for four generations. I combed Bill Miller for a neighborly hair but could find none. He wanted them gone. I was confused. Where was the congenial, collaborative person I had met at the conference a few years ago? Like a good mediator, I did some reality testing, asking him to think about the next landowner who might replace the Scholeses. But Bill could imagine no greater threat than this elderly pair of bird-watchers driving through his land.

The Scholeses had assumed they would use the easement through the Miller property because the only other access was a thirty-five-mile dirt road over a mountain pass that had not been used for decades and as a result had almost disappeared. After a rain, however, the seven-mile Miller road was almost as impassable, with deep ruts and gullies. The Scholeses' old Land Cruiser leaped and bucked like a rodeo bull as Bob picked his way along, hoping they would both arrive safely, with no broken bones. Every mile or so, one of them would have to rappel down from the Land Cruiser to the ground and open one of the six gates while the other drove through. Then whichever of them was gatekeeper would have to close the gate and hoist himself or herself back up into the high-clearance vehicle, strapping in for the next lurching stretch to the next gate. The Scholeses offered to pay for grading and surfacing the road and installing cattle guards, but Bill Miller had a host of reasons for saying no: the weather, liability issues, disturbance to cattle, and so on. The Scholeses wanted guests to be able to visit them, but Bill had once threatened would-be visitors, they said, with a shotgun.

In frustration, the Scholeses had finally sued the Millers, in both Arizona and New Mexico, and that really set the lion on a rampage. Different fine points in the cases were decided in conflicting ways, but fearing a future decision might favor the Scholeses, Bill agreed to mediation. Tired of the expense and hassle of the suits, the Scholeses were ready for any solution. At least the mediator would come to them; they wouldn't have to drive those seven nightmarish miles to go to court or to see a lawyer.

So into this turbulent scene I drove, over a deeply gullied dirt road, to spend time with each couple. At their core, the Scholeses admitted, they did not like cattle and did not understand the ranching way of life. They dreamed of a landscape restored to its natural, cattle-free state and proudly pointed to the land on their side of the fence, cattle free for twenty years, in contrast with the other side, where the Millers' cattle grazed. (Truthfully, sometimes it was hard for me to see the difference.) They knew they had a legal right to cross the ranchland, and they were no more interested in a neighborly relationship than the Millers were.

In talking with Bill and Carrol, I learned they wanted to limit the number of guests traveling the road because they saw strangers as inherently dangerous. There were illegals coming across from Mexico, and you just didn't know who might pop up on that road. They were also concerned that there might be an accident during the roadwork and that the contractor might not have the appropriate license and liability insurance. They were worried that their cattle would be upset—cattle were actually quite delicate animals, Bill explained. As for surfacing the road, how hypocritical of these so-called environmentalists to want to bring all kinds of toxic materials onto the land!

This was the only case I have ever had in which I met with the parties separately. One reason to separate parties is if one has all the power, as in some domestic abuse cases. Equitable negotiations are impossible when one person lives in terror of the other; the prey will settle for anything to try to keep the predator at bay. But in this case, each side had its own power. Bill Miller was intimidating in size, personality, and history with the land and community. And the Scholeses had their own kind of power, which included the law, probably on their side.

In truth, I was afraid of the hatred and resentment that would explode from both sides and the resulting fallout for all of us. It was easier to deal with the Millers and the Scholeses separately, to listen to each rant about the other, to delicately try to propose looking at it from the other's point of view, and to receive the negative blast myself.

After the initial meeting with each couple, I drafted an agreement for them to consider. Both sides insisted on many changes. I incorporated the changes and sent it back to them. It came back with comments again, from both. I redrafted the agreement and went down for a visit. In all, there were seven drafts—maybe one for each mile—and in the end I called it quits. I went down for one last visit to suggest that we refer the dispute to a local retired judge who had agreed to act as an arbitrator.

The Scholeses were gracious as ever, inviting me into their rambling but cozy house, wallpapered with bird photos and art. They were full of news about bird sightings. They showed me a picture in a bird book of a rare species of hummingbird they had seen the day before, and then we went outside to see where they were planning to set out more bird feeders and houses. Katie, small and birdlike herself, led me around the yard, picking her way carefully, darting her head this way and that, always on the lookout for a bird or an animal. She held her binoculars at the ready just in case. Bob, who had been a pilot in World War II, was a handsome man, upright and sturdy, shadowing Katie with a loving concern. They were looking forward to a visit from their daughter and her family the next week. Of course, they were worried that Bill would mistake their relatives for illegals and give them trouble.

We came back inside, and over iced tea they agreed that the mediation was going nowhere and they were ready for arbitration. They just wanted to be done with it and get the road graded. They asked if I could be the arbitrator, and I explained that it would not be appropriate when I had been working as a mediator, and that I really was not comfortable in that role. I wanted to help people find their own solution, not impose one on them. They understood. I wished them well, and we parted friends.

I bounced along the road back toward the highway, stopping to talk with Bill and Carrol Miller about the next step. They, too, were gracious. I had more iced tea and sat in a big wicker chair on their wide veranda looking out over the valley, the road twisting away in the distance. I explained that I had contacted the retired judge whom Bill had recommended and who was happy to help. They agreed to abide by his decision. We sat awhile and talked about the increase in illegal traffic across the border, about the price of cattle and the lack of rain. Bill told me about the javelina he had killed—meanest animal around, he said. It had been coming out from behind the jagged rock formation near his house, and he shot it from the veranda. He actually shuddered when he thought about it, and I realized that it was possible for Bill Miller to be afraid. The sun was sinking, beginning to light up the Peloncillos from the west. I knew I should get on the road, but the view was so beautiful, the vastness so quiet, I wanted to stay a little longer. Carrol had gone inside to start dinner. Bill and I enjoyed the silence together.

And then he broke it, in an uncharacteristically soft voice. "I used to have twelve hummingbird feeders hanging up there," he said, pointing to a rafter running along the front of the porch. "My grandpa had twelve, and I just kept up the tradition. Used to love to watch those birds."

"What happened to the feeders?" I looked around. "Where did they go?"

"Took 'em down." His voice had a faraway note to it.

Silence.

"Why?" I was mystified.

"Ever since they moved in," he said, tossing his head in the direction of the Scholeses' place, "just can't enjoy 'em any more."

"Bill, that's terrible. That's so sad." I was shocked that he would deprive himself of something pleasurable, a part of his natural landscape. "That is really sad," I repeated as it dawned on me. He couldn't enjoy anything that the enemy enjoyed. He would rather do without than share that small piece of common ground, the beauty of a hummingbird, with the Scholeses.

"Sure is sad. You're right about that." His voice was strong again. He looked straight ahead, out toward the rutted road. I realized that he was referring to the fact that the Scholeses had moved in, with their East Coast, litigious, educated ways, and by their very presence had robbed him of the hummingbirds. As I drove away from the ranch house, I felt profoundly sad. I still do when I think about it.

The arbitration with the judge failed, and the Scholeses eventually took the Millers to court again, this time receiving a clear verdict giving them the right to use the easement through the Miller property. Katie Scholes died in June 2012. In his mid-nineties and quite frail, Bob remains on the property, now a research center and covered by a conservation easement. Bill keeps an eye on the traffic through his land, by some accounts with a shotgun at the ready, although the sharp increase in illegal crossings from Mexico may have given him another reason to be armed. The road is not improved, nor are the relations.

Looking back, I wonder what possessed me to take the case and stick with it through seven iterations of an agreement. Surely I saw the depth of emotion, the immutability of the Millers' position early on, but I barged ahead. We mediators do that all the time—take cases that are doomed. Being asked to rescue an impossible situation flatters the ego. We like to think we can make it better, overcome any barrier, create relationships out of hostility.

In this case, I suppose I was under the spell of Bill Miller the storyteller, whom I had heard talk about the beginning of the Malpai Borderlands Group. During my time with him, I wondered how the same person who had been a leader of this groundbreaking alliance between ranchers and environmentalists could balk at an agreement with a neighbor that seemed, at least to the outsider, to be a simple solution to a straightforward problem. But we are complex creatures, and the Bill Miller who was the neighbor of the Scholeses was not a seeker of solutions, not a potential partner for a greater good. He was angry, defensive, and frightened—frightened that his livelihood and his way of life were endangered, just like the life of the Chiricahua leopard frog. The Scholeses personified the threat, and unwittingly they played the part he cast them in.

We are able at some times and in some places to open up to new ideas, to take courageous steps. But we do not give up that place deep in ourselves where fear, resentment, and prejudice live—remnants of our personal traumas or perhaps the legacy of our cultural and historical past. Bill Miller could look for the common ground in the context of the Malpai Borderlands Group, but when it came to his bird-watching neighbors, so close to where he lived—not just physically but also emotionally—the lion sprang from that deep place, and agreement was impossible.

For those of us in the conflict resolution field, it is important to understand the complexity not just of the coalitions we may be working with but also of each individual. Given the right circumstances, we are all capable at some level of being collaborative, just as we are all vulnerable to burrowing deep into that place of hurt and fear. The best we can do, whether as mediators or as parties in conflict, is to acknowledge that part of ourselves, come to know it, and recognize when our lion—or our neighbor's lion—leaps to the surface.

So I must accept that Bill Miller, the stubborn, angry neighbor, is also capable of commitment to the principles of the Malpai Borderlands Group, and today the Boot Heel is a better place for it. The group's accomplishments are impressive and include a 2004 safe harbor agreement with the US Fish and Wildlife Service to provide protection for endangered species on private ranch land and a multispecies habitat conservation plan in 2008 covering hundreds of thousands of acres of Chihuahuan Desert landscape. The group's goal is "to restore and maintain the natural processes that create and protect a healthy, unfragmented landscape to support a diverse, flourishing community of human, plant and animal life in our borderlands region." Members will work toward these goals, they say, by encouraging profitable ranching and other traditional livelihoods, which will sustain the open land for generations to come. Malpai members continue to tell their story around the country at events of all kinds, and that image of a cattle-punching cowboy carrying water for the little spotted frog has been very effective in building support for their cause. Their partners now include federal and state land and wildlife management agencies, university research programs, and several environmental organizations.

And the Malpai Borderlands Group is not alone. There are dozens of coalitions around the West and probably the nation with similar goals, some contemporary with the Malpai group, with founding dates in the early and mid-1990s. One of the earliest was the Applegate Partnership—now the Applegate Partnership and Watershed Council—founded by a group of private and federal interests to deal with the "lizards versus logs" conflicts that were tearing a rural Oregon community apart. Group members believed that natural resource management and environmental quality were not mutually exclusive, and their success bears that out.

The Valle Grande Grass Bank in northern New Mexico is another innovative partnership. Inspired by the Malpai grass bank, William deBuys, local author, hay farmer, and Southwest representative of The Conservation Fund, worked with Palemon Martinez of the Northern New Mexico Stockmen's Association and the US Department of Agriculture's Cooperative

Extension Service and Forest Service to establish a grass bank on a 36,000-acre national forest grazing allotment, where permittees might send their cattle to "summer camp" while their home allotments get a little badly needed R&R by way of rest, prescribed fire, and other treatments.

Another shining example, based in Santa Fe, is the Quivira Coalition. The founders' goal was to nurture what they saw as "an emerging radical center" that included ranchers, conservationists, scientists, and public land managers who believed that ecologically sensitive land management was compatible with economically robust ranches. The inspiration of Barbara Johnson and Courtney White, the coalition has to date worked to restore over 1 million acres and many miles of stream banks. Its annual conference draws hundreds from around the West, and I am always in the crowd.

I know there are those on both the ranching and the environmental sides who deeply resent these collaborative efforts. They feel that their respective leaders have consorted with the enemy, given in on important points, and settled for too little. I have heard from some of them over the years, and their emotions rival those of the Millers and the Scholeses. A particularly passionate environmentalist friend rails against both the ranchers and the environmentalists who participate in the Malpai Borderlands Group and the Quivira Coalition. He claims that the ranchers are conniving and manipulative, the environmentalists are dupes and wimps, and these "so-called collaborations" compromise environmental values and damage resources. And one does not have to go far to find a hard-core rancher whose hatred of environmentalists makes any thought of a joint project impossible.

But I am a mediator, and to me partnerships such as the Malpai Borderlands Group, the Applegate Partnership and Watershed Council, the Valle Grande Grass Bank, and the Quivira Coalition are inspiring. Sure, the actions are strategic and designed to benefit your team, but if you can multiply those on your team by finding others who will benefit, who cares what label they bring with them? These projects have resulted in dozens of ranchers, environmentalists, researchers, and federal and state land managers now knowing, respecting, and maybe even enjoying one another's company as they work together to preserve a beautiful part of the country. Whether or not any of them are ready to be neighbors is another question.

CHAPTER EIGHT

So Close to Consensus

Did you know that chain saws, leaf blowers, scooters, and dozens of other small, noisy items have two-stroke engines and that cars and trucks have four-stroke engines? That was all news to me when I was asked to help the US Environmental Protection Agency (EPA) develop regulations for air emissions from two-stroke engines. This goes to show just how ignorant your mediator or facilitator may be. But after all, I told myself, I don't need to be the expert. I just need to be able to handle the people. Ah, yes, let me repeat that—just be able to handle the people.

To keep from totally embarrassing myself, I asked a friend to give me a quick tutorial in engines. (This was pre-Internet, and it was either call a friend or go to the library.) We sat over margaritas and he drew schemata on napkins while I took copious notes. What I learned was this. Two-stroke engines work great for small equipment because they are light, compact, and cheap. Like a car, a chain saw has an internal combustion engine, but it fires at every revolution of the piston instead of every other revolution as a car does, giving an extra power boost from a smaller source. Another big advantage is that two-stroke engines work in any orientation. You can hold them sideways or upside down and the oil will still flow. But two-stroke engines are dirty. If you operate a weed whacker for one hour, you produce more air pollution than if you drove your car for 450 miles. Because the lubricating oil and the fuel are mixed together, when they burn—and they often burn incompletely—they emit much more soot (particulate matter) and hydrocarbons than do their four-stroke cousins. However, since nothing is ever simple, they may emit less carbon monoxide and fewer nitrogen oxides.

And now you know as much about small engines as I did when I welcomed the newly formed Negotiated Rulemaking Advisory Committee for Small Nonroad Engine Regulations to its first meeting in Ann Arbor, Michigan, home of the EPA's emissions-testing facility. The group, which included EPA policy makers and technical staff as well as environmental and industry representatives, was charged with developing a set of air emission regulations for two-stroke non-road engines—by consensus.

"Consensus" is a dangerous word. It can mean many things to many people, and those meanings can change during the course of a negotiation, depending how things are going for your side at any given moment. If you've got the majority behind you, then you might prefer to have a nice, clean vote rather than to struggle through a tortured debate to try to reach agreement. If, however, you are a holdout on a point that is not popular with the rest of the group, you will treasure consensus and press for a definition that requires unanimity. For this reason, I am always very careful to help the members of a group define exactly what they mean by consensus at the beginning of the process and make sure they stick with it to the end.

In this case, I felt consensus needed to require unanimity. In creating the advisory committee, we had worked with the EPA to make the group as small as possible. The greater the number at the table, the more egos there are to deal with, the more time can be wasted, and the more money can be spent. It is easier to help a small group develop rapport and, one hopes, a degree of trust—keys to reaching an agreement. The challenge is to create as small a group as possible while still ensuring full representation of interests. If a single person or organization can speak for a certain interest, there is no need for more than one representative at the table. In this case, we decided that health and environment could be represented, respectively, by the American Lung Association and the Natural Resources Defense Council (NRDC). On the other hand, the business and industry interests were harder to reduce to a single spokesperson. Clearly, the Truck and Engine Manufacturers Association deserved a seat. The equipment manufacturers needed three seats, given the wide range of products, some handheld, some not. One seat represented the interests of the dealers who sold and serviced the equipment and engines, and a manufacturer of emissions control devices got a seat. A seat was given to the State of Wisconsin, home of several engine and equipment companies, and another seat went to a national organization representing state regulatory agencies. These last two would have to adapt to the new federal regulations. With one seat for the EPA, that made a total of eleven, a good number for constructive discussion on a complex topic.

This seeming imbalance of "votes" in the process—two out of eleven on the health and environment side—was naturally a concern for the American Lung Association and the NRDC. Even if they counted the EPA as an environmental voice, which for them was not necessarily a given, they were a very small minority. They wanted equal numbers to keep from being outvoted on critical issues, but, we pointed out, if all decisions are made by consensus the numbers at the table won't matter. One single voice can block agreement; all voices, big and small, have equal power. It was important, we added, that no fallback to a vote be built into the process. Even a vote that required a super-supermajority, such as 80 percent, would undermine the minority voices at the table. The group agreed to unanimous consensus with no fallback vote; one dissenter and there would be no consensus.

There was great incentive for the group to reach consensus: if they did, those regulations they had agreed on would be put forth by the EPA without change. In other words, if the members could agree, the committee had the power to write the agency's regulations—a very tantalizing possibility for those at the table. Failing consensus, the job of writing and promulgating regulations would revert to the EPA, and it would be business as usual.

At our first meeting, in September 1993, committee members introduced themselves and identified their particular interests in the regulation of small engines. The engine and equipment manufacturers and their dealers—all represented by associations—were a jovial bunch, great salesmen and sharp attorneys with an easy, amiable way about them. Of course, beneath that exterior was a fierce commitment to preserving the right of those companies to continue to make a good profit while providing their customers with the goods they desired. They had technical studies, legal arguments, even moral justification to defend these rights, essentially the right to pollute. Eager to ingratiate themselves with the group, they spoke enthusiastically about how they were looking forward to this process, were sure they had a lot to offer, and were eager to educate the group about the value of their products, the needs of business, and the truth about emissions.

The introductions moved around the U-shaped table, eventually coming to the attorney for the Portable Power Equipment Manufacturers Association. He said that, like everyone else, he was certainly interested in cleaner air, and he knew there were ways to achieve that goal while protecting the rights of his clients, the equipment manufacturers. He was followed by Elaine. There was nothing jovial or even pleasant about Elaine. She was all business, a young Washington, DC, lawyer with a major environmental organization. When I nodded to her, indicating it was her turn to introduce herself, she stared straight ahead and said, "I am an attorney with the NRDC, and I am here representing all things that breathe on the planet." Shooting a cold glance at the previous speaker, seated next to her, she added, "Those are *my* clients." I waited for a little something more, an acknowledgment of the rest of the group, of the challenge that lay ahead, anything. But she was done. She looked at me briefly with raised eyebrows, as if to say, "What more do you want? This is who I am." There was a little buzz around the table. Her eyes narrowed behind her tortoiseshell glasses. Bright and obviously committed, she was probably an excellent litigator, but I worried about her role in this process. Would she be able to engage with the group? Could she really listen, debate, and negotiate? Would she ever smile?

The committee had been organized under the Federal Advisory Committee Act, or FACA, which was enacted to ensure that no one sector of the public has inappropriate influence on a government agency making a decision. The 1972 act requires any agency or department seeking advice from the private sector to do so in a prescribed forum, the FACA committee. The committee must have a balance of all the interests—not just industry, not just environmental, but representation of all interests. Meetings must be open to the public. Each committee must draft its own charter (which must be approved by Congress) describing its purpose and explaining how it will operate in a manner that is equitable for all the members. The FACA committee must be facilitated by a third party and must make decisions by consensus. The agency must provide resources to support the needs of the committee, including facilitation, travel expenses for members, and technical support. All this is overwhelming for many stressed-out bureaucrats who see FACA as time-consuming and loaded with burdensome requirements.

But perhaps the real reason for "FACA phobia" is that FACA brings bureaucrats face-to-face with their impacted publics. Instead of simply writing pages of technical language in a cozy cubicle out of sight of the civilian world, policy and technical staff must hash through every pro, every con, and everything in between with a group that includes those who are established critics of the agency and probably enemies of one another. In addition, the knowledge level at the table will vary dramatically. Some committee members may be very sophisticated on the technical and legal issues, perhaps even more so than the agency staff. Others may be stakeholders with a lot to lose or gain in the negotiations but little understanding of the complexities. What makes all this heterogeneity especially scary is that it will lead to fireworks and strong emotions at the table, the last things a quiet, nerdy rule writer wants to deal with.

I am a FACA fan. I think it's a great way to safeguard against special interests influencing decisions—such as the development of rules and regulations—made by the executive branch of government. All those with a stake in the issue at question can communicate on an equal basis with the decision makers, sharing their knowledge with the agency in an open and equitable way. The result is an agency with a rich, balanced body of knowledge as it moves forward. And as for facing an unpleasant bunch of constituents, that's what I'm there for.

So, as required by FACA, at our first meeting we adopted a set of protocols that included a mission statement, a press policy, a process for record keeping, our definition of consensus (unanimity), the responsibilities of committee members, the agency, and the facilitators, and much more. To better tackle the complex issues that lay ahead, we also created four task groups: Test Procedure, Technology, Certification, and Public Education and Market Incentives.

Developing the regulations took a grueling two and a half years.

Although we planned on quarterly meetings, additional meetings were often plugged in to try to speed the process along. Each meeting was filled with technical jargon, legal wrangling, hand-wringing, fist pounding, brow sweating, and cajoling. When the EPA announced that there was funding to take us all to the National Lawn and Garden Show in Louisville, Kentucky, to see the latest in technology and its applications, we cheered like fourth graders being rewarded with a field trip after doing well on a math test. It was a gigantic engine- and exhaust-filled event, where we all—except Elaine—test-drove the latest-model lawn mowers around on the ridiculously lush grass, had our pictures taken with a giant cutout Paul Bunyan, and feasted on all things barbecued.

And there were moments when our relationships became personal, when a ray of real life shone on us. The EPA committee member had a baby during year one, and by the time we finished she was pregnant again. Three became grandparents. Another traveled to China to adopt a baby girl. We passed pictures around the table, and there was much cooing. And there were tragedies. An enormous earthquake hit Kobe, Japan, in January 1995 and destroyed the massive Kawasaki plant, an obvious impact to the company's bottom line. The loss felt at the table, however, was of colleagues and friends.

But the vast majority of hours were spent struggling to understand emissions studies and technical presentations, to complete work group assignments before the next meeting, to sort out the critical issues from the less important, to figure out what trade-offs would lead to the most gain all around, to articulate potential points of consensus in concise, clear language. My struggle as lead facilitator was to follow the substance of the discussion, keep the group moving through each overstuffed agenda, and intuit when one or more members was about to implode, or explode, depending on the personality.

These were extremely complex issues involving both the technology of small engines—carburetors, design, configuration, and so on—and the chemistry of emissions. The rule had to cover many different engine types and hundreds of handheld and non-handheld applications. The committee members, with their different levels of knowledge and experience, had to master a wide range of emissions-reducing strategies, including standards for both exhaust from engines and evaporative emissions from spillages; mandatory and voluntary programs; testing, compliance, and enforcement programs; and public education programs. Given all these complexities, the committee members would have been wise to focus on policy and overarching principles and entrust the details to the technicians. But their appetite for detail was insatiable, and they were sure that one more set of data would make the difference and lead the way to agreement. Yet each additional test or study simply became another focus for suspicion and confusion.

Many had come to the table hoping that their particular product could be excluded from the new regulations. Certain products used in public safety contexts, for instance, were excluded without much debate. The representative of the ice auger manufacturers had a tougher sell. He argued, unsuccessfully, that because nitrogen oxide emissions from a two-stroke engine were much lower in cold weather than in warm weather, his ice augers (used for ice fishing) and snowblowers should be excluded from the regulation. The representatives who failed to gain exclusion focused on the issues that would affect their bottom lines the most: testing of engines and equipment for compliance, certification, timing of the introduction of the new standards, and, of course, the standards themselves.

In spite of our efforts to balance the power, there were inequities at the table. Consensus gave equal power to all when it came to decision making. But the reality was that industry and business had the resources, the time, the knowledge, and the motivation to take an active role in the development of data, analysis of issues, and discussion of proposals. The EPA was grateful for the access to additional resources and expertise that it could not afford. In fact, gaining that access was probably one of the agency's reasons for creating a FACA committee. Others, particularly the environmental, public health, and state representatives, were stretched thin in terms of money, time, and expertise. Furthermore, business and industry had a very deep bench. Each of their committee members had an alternate; the other members could not afford alternates. If the committee member was not at a meeting, he or she had to try to catch up for the next meeting, and catching up was tough, given the volume of information and the complexity of the issues.

There was another difference among the parties: motivation. For industry representatives, the motivation to be at the table was to protect jobs and profits as much as possible, ensuring environmental compliance while building in flexibility for their corporations in meeting standards. Their stakes were personal and direct—loss of job, loss of profit, loss of a place in the market. If their engines and equipment could not be built to meet new emissions standards, they would be out of business. The market would turn to other products—electric, maybe, or four-stroke designs—or to new technologies (which our associations emphasized were very expensive and many years away).

At stake for the environmental and health interests, including the state committee members, was the health of the planet—a more theoretical and less personal motivation. Passionate as they were about their cause, they were not going to be personally affected by the outcome any more than would any other living thing that breathes. If they "lost" in the negotiation, they would not lose their jobs; their lives presumably would be unchanged. Industry representatives, with their livelihoods at stake, were energetic in tackling the problem. The environmental and health representatives were passionate, but that personal urgency was lacking. These differences in perspective and values were difficult to discuss, but their influence on how members communicated with and felt about one another was profound. I noted a curious parallel between the industry representatives at the table and those Hispanic villagers in northern New Mexico (chapter 4). Both groups had their livelihood to lose, and both groups saw the environmentalists as unrealistic, righteous, and without a real stake in the conflict.

Individual companies, such as Toro, Lawn-Boy, Stihl, Ryobi, and many more, faithfully attended the meetings at their own expense to track the committee's progress. They would have loved to have a seat at the table, but it would have been impossible to choose among them and unfair to ask one to represent competing companies. So dozens of companies took a watchdog role with respect to their member associations, with their lawyers and scientists and chief executive officers in the audience hanging on every word and taking copious notes. Twice during each meeting they were allowed to address the committee, and they used this opportunity to remind their representatives at the negotiating table where their loyalties should lie. The result was that those at the table could never speak as openly and creatively as I would have liked—not with that Greek chorus of weed whackers in the audience. The industry leads onstage had to be very careful to demonstrate their hard-line, take-no-prisoners stance.

As with any high-profile case, external events—political, economic, legal—affected our process. The Sierra Club had sued the EPA for not implementing the 1990 amendments to the Clean Air Act, and the court order to publish small-engine regulations by April 1996 was a motivator in the creation of our advisory committee. But of course that recent history also stoked general resentment against environmentalists, whom the business and industry side saw as unreasonable and litigious. When we began our meetings in 1993, the pendulum had swung toward the environmental side. But with the Republican landslide in the midterm election of 1994, it careened in the other direction. Our first meeting after the election saw the industry and business committee members beaming, unable to contain themselves. No longer on the defensive, they charged ahead. Our process was the same—same mission, same data, same studies, same models, same laws—but the political context was entirely different. Gladys, the representative from the American Lung Association, and Elaine, from the NRDC, came into that meeting tired and stretched too thin, as usual, but with a new look of concern in their eyes.

With the April 1996 court-ordered deadline looming, we pushed to finish our final committee statement, which was to be our consensus document. Unable to agree on all parts of the regulations, and never ready to give up the search for more data, members decided to seek consensus on their progress so far, hoping that the EPA would take seriously their product as it moved forward.

The first part of the document was an agreement in principle, to be signed by each member, which explained the process and clarified the role of committee members when the rule was made public. The principles were expressed in heavyweight legalistic language, which I will spare you. Significantly, the EPA pledged to base its rule on the work of the committee and to continue to consult with the committee and let the members review the draft rule prior to publication. In return, each member was expected to uphold, defend, and not file suit against the EPA rule if it comported with the committee's outline for the rule. If another party filed suit, all the members would file memoranda with the court explaining their participation in this process and their support of the rule as written.

This kind of language was standard in negotiated rule making. It was important that participants in the process not cut and run, that they remain supportive and open about their own roles in developing the rule.

The second part of the document was a draft outline for the proposed rule. Clearly, it was impossible for our group to craft the actual language of the regulations, but the outline would give a foundation for the regulations. It was organized by topic: applicability, effective date, engine classification, standards, test procedures, compliance, in-use program, imports, public education and marketing, certification, and dealer responsibility. Some of the items were quite specific, offering numbers and dates; others were more general.

By the end of our process we were exhausted and somewhat disappointed by our failure to do more, but the real possibility of consensus on the agreement in principle and the draft outline spurred us on. The EPA boosted our energy by saying that consensus on this document would be extremely useful in the agency's next steps.

At our last meeting, on February 16, 1996, I went around the table and sought consensus on the document. Committee members chose to tackle the substance, the draft outline, and then come back and consider the agreement in principle. I suggested that we seek consensus on the draft outline as a whole, but I was dreaming. Members wanted to go through each of the eleven sections. Different parts had been crafted by different task groups, and not all members were equally familiar with all parts. The first section, "Applicability," covered those products that would be excluded from the regulations. We had spent a lot of time on this, and I thought it would be relatively simple. To my delight, there was one nod after another as we went around the table.

But my delight faded when I reached Elaine and saw her head shake in the negative. There were groans. I asked her to explain her objection. She said she could not support this section that provided loopholes for certain products that she thought should be regulated. There was a brief discussion to probe the potential for an agreement, after which I asked her again, suggesting that she offer alternative language. Again, her head shook. No alternative language. No consensus. We soldiered through one section after another, and it became clear that Elaine was not going to offer consensus on anything.

I was not the only one in despair. Although Elaine had never been a happy camper, we had all had reason to hope that she could live with the agreement. Other committee members accepted the fact that they were not going to get their dream regulations, and the understanding was that you offered consensus if you could "live with the document as a whole," in other words, if there was enough good to make it worthwhile and nothing bad enough to merit a veto. But for Elaine, nothing could be "lived with."

When we came to the section on public education and marketing, I dug in my heels. Elaine had served on this task group and had been instrumental in convincing the manufacturers to accept a labeling program for small-engine products. Chain saws, lawn mowers, weed whackers, and the like would be labeled with a tag indicating the product's level of pollution. Although the task group had not been specific, the idea was that a tag might have a green tree symbol if its emissions were low, even two or three trees to indicate greater reductions. This was a way of offering manufacturers an incentive to strive for better, cleaner technology. They had agreed reluctantly. I asked for consensus on this section. All heads nodded until we got around the table to Elaine. I was dumbfounded. How could she object to a labeling program that would encourage consumers to buy cleaner products? I tried to control myself.

"Elaine, I don't understand. What is your objection to this section on consumer education? We talked a long time about a green tree labeling program."

"I don't like the idea of pretending that there is anything clean about these engines. There isn't. They are polluters. It offends me to put a tree on a polluting machine."

I could see that we were not going to reach consensus on anything, and I was frustrated. No, I was angry. A mediator can't help but want consensus. If I didn't have consensus, at least I could get a little revenge.

"So, Elaine, I really am confused here. I can't believe you would oppose something that would promote a cleaner environment." I shook my head in bewilderment, as if I didn't know the truth, that she was simply acting in bad faith, that she had sat through hours and hours of negotiations, never from day one intending to agree to anything unless it banned two-stroke engines from the face of the earth. I pretended to play the role of the patient mediator, still searching for the elusive common ground.

"So let me try this out. If the labels could somehow show that one product was dirtier than another, rather than cleaner than another, could you agree to that?" She blinked at me rapidly through her glasses, her lips sealed shut. "For instance, if the labels had black smoke clouds on them—three black clouds for the dirtiest, two for less dirty, and one for least dirty—would that work for you?"

She didn't even hesitate. "No. I would not agree to that."

I wanted to have a tantrum right there, the kind where you stamp your feet, ball your hands into fists and pound the air, scrunch up your face, and let out a high-pitched squeal. But instead I took a deep breath and tried to bring the years of work to a close with some grace. I acknowledged that we had not reached consensus on our document, and that it was now the task of the EPA to draft regulations. How fortunate, I added, that EPA representatives had been at our table from the beginning and had participated as full members of the committee. The agency staff could make use of all our work, with full understanding of all the points of view expressed during the process. The EPA spokesperson said, yes, indeed, they had all received a very valuable education on the subject and were grateful for the time and effort put in by all the committee members. We all went through these perfunctory appreciations, but I could tell that I wasn't the only one confused and disappointed.

The agency did in fact promulgate regulations that mirrored closely the work of the committee. Even without consensus at the end, the effort had been worthwhile. And I had had my first brush with bad faith. There would be others, but the first is always the worst.

I should not have been surprised by Elaine's subterfuge. Early on I had talked to her privately about her willingness and ability to play a cooperative role in the process. I reminded her of the good faith clause in the protocols, which she had signed at the first meeting. She responded that she would attend meetings and participate on behalf of her organization. Period. Later, when her behavior gave us concern, my colleague in the case, John Folk-Williams, called her executive director to discuss whether or not she was the best representative for her organization. The answer was yes, she was their choice, the right one to be at the table.

It is the role of the mediator to ensure (as much as possible) that the right people are at the table. This means those who can represent their interest, who have some degree of authority, who can communicate clearly and with respect, and who are participating in good faith, willing to consider a variety of solutions to the mutual problem. Before the selection is made, the mediator usually talks with the responsible person to suggest these criteria and answer questions about the process. But the selection of the representative at the table is the responsibility and right of the organization, company, agency, or other entity. Once the group has been formed, it is very difficult to remove or replace a member.

Burned by Elaine, I saw her as a "bad apple," uncooperative in the mediation process, someone whose beliefs and commitments are so deeply held as to prevent any real negotiation or even consideration of other points of view. But there are other possibilities. I have seen environmental activists unable to offer consensus not because they believe the agreement is lacking but because their board, or membership, or boss has told them to hold the hard line no matter what. Having been through a long and arduous process with adversaries and allies, the person at the table may have come to realize the wisdom in the proposal but still be under instructions to veto.

I do not know the background of Elaine's refusal to offer consensus, whether she was simply a self-righteous personality, as I assumed, or whether she was acting under orders from above. I was so frustrated that I didn't bother to try and find out. I have lingering questions, though, about how to handle a difficult participant who may be acting in bad faith. Could we have screened out Elaine in the beginning, before the process began? Perhaps. Should we have? That is a harder question for me. It doesn't feel fair to exclude from the process those with the most strongly held beliefs, even if at the end of some days I might wish I had. It is a dilemma most mediators face at some point, and there is no right answer.

CHAPTER NINE

When the Past Won't Go Away

Public policy mediators and their clients are always looking for ways to evaluate the success of their processes. Besides wanting the best possible result for the interests at table, the profession naturally would like to claim victory, and the client would like to show money well spent. But as you have already seen, these processes are complex, and at any given moment, in any given meeting room, the evaluation could be A+ or D–. So, are there standards that we can use to measure the value of the outcome?

Mediation students are taught that a successful agreement provides satisfaction for participants in three equally important areas: substantive, process, and psychological. Substantive satisfaction means that you can live with the agreement and you believe that it will be effective and long lasting. It is your best option, even if it is not perfect. Process satisfaction means that you feel the process was fair, efficient, and well designed. The right people were at the table, and the mediator did a decent job. Finally, there is psychological satisfaction. Although it is hard to define, I see psychological satisfaction as what is left over after the participant evaluates the substance and the process. You ask yourself, "How do I feel?" Do you feel satisfied with the role you played and how you played it? Were you treated with respect? Did the others at the table and the mediator understand what you needed and perhaps even have some empathy for you? Was there that human connection that can be key to finding common ground? Although it is not perfect, I think this classic evaluation tool is especially useful as the process evolves. Both the mediator and the participants can check the three areas and make adjustments, ending, it is hoped, on a harmonious note. The case that follows is an example of both the harmony and the cacophony that can be found as strong personalities deal with difficult issues of the past, present, and future.

Although most Indian students today go to public schools, both on and off the reservation, there remain 156 schools throughout the United States that are funded by the federal Bureau of Indian Affairs (BIA). A few of these are BIA boarding or day schools; others are run by a tribe or a tribal community. They are scattered throughout the country and range in size from fewer than a hundred students to over a thousand. They are a legacy from the treaty promise to provide education for all Indian students. At that time, the government assumption was that the Indians' traditional way of life was already a thing of the past and that the sooner these students were educated in "white" ways and assimilated into the mainstream melting pot (to mix metaphors), the better for all involved. The early schools were boarding facilities, and they are, unfortunately, best known for documented abuse at the hands of BIA educators.

These schools—like all their public school counterparts throughout the country—are subject to the No Child Left Behind Act of 2001, but clearly have special characteristics that require special attention. In 2003 the US Secretary of the Interior mandated that the regulations governing the BIA-funded schools should be in compliance with the No Child Left Behind Act by the beginning of the 2004 school year. The time line was extremely ambitious: craft six separate regulations governing financing, student rights, performance measures, and other crucial aspects of school governance in five months. Most projects of such scope and complexity take years.

And not only was the clock running at unreasonable speed, the BIA, as always, was under enormous pressure from Indian country. Knowing its every move would be scrutinized and criticized, the bureau decided to draft the regulations in an open—"transparent" was the word of the day—process that included representatives of the tribes and schools that would be affected as well as government staff. And the bureau decided to operate by consensus in order to be sure that every voice at the negotiating table would have equal weight. To do this, the agency invoked the Federal Advisory Committee Act (FACA) and formed a FACA committee, as the Environmental Protection Agency did in its small-engine regulatory negotiation (chapter 8). As is the case with most agencies, staffers knew it would be easier to write the regulations in the privacy of their own cubicles, but the public pressure on the process was enormous and they understood that doing the work together in a public forum was the right thing to do. And, as with the EPA negotiations, most of the federal representatives came with some anxiety about doing their work in public and under the collaborative umbrella.

The committee of twenty-two included eleven representatives of the US Department of the Interior's Bureau of Indian Affairs (policy makers, lawyers, analysts, and regional administrators) and eleven representatives of Indian country (tribal officials, school staff, teachers, parents, and board members) who had been selected in an elaborate process from a pool of nominees. But the lines were inevitably fuzzy. The federal side included two enrolled tribal members, and there were two Anglos on the tribal side, a school principal and a teacher.

Although my focus had been on natural resources disputes, I was hired to manage the process, I believe, because of my credibility in Indian country. I guided the selection of committee members, balancing the group in terms of geography, size and type of school, and diversity of school positions. And so that I would be as prepared as possible, I talked to most of the members, tribal and federal, prior to our first meeting.

The only way I saw of possibly meeting the deadline was to negotiate concurrently the six regulations, letting small groups draft documents for review and, I hoped, consensus by the committee as a whole. I negotiated with the agency for five additional facilitators to handle the small groups. Since Western Network had dissolved in 1999, I had been in business as Lucy Moore Associates, Inc., doing the same work on my own. To keep my work life simple, I had no employees, instead subcontracting with colleagues when I needed help. In this case, given the makeup of the committee, I felt it was important to have diversity in the facilitation team. Including me, our team of six included three men and three women; two were Hispanic, two Anglo, one Navajo, and one *Mexicana*. Even better, they were all friends with whom I had wanted to work for years. All the hassle of bookkeeping, administration, and keeping track of the flock was well worth it.

Three of the six rules had to do with funding allocations and disbursements and were very complex. The fourth dealt with geographic boundaries for schools and who should have the authority to determine what student went to which school in situations where there was a choice between public, private, BIA, and tribal. Should the parent decide? Or should the child go to the closest school? How could students be prevented from shuffling from one school to another to avoid discipline or to take advantage of an athletic season or a powwow? And what about bus routes? An insight I gained during the process was that some Indian families were very loyal to a certain boarding school. Even if they lived next door to a public school, they might prefer to send their children to a boarding school, even one in another state. "That is where our family has always gone, and that is where we want our children to go," said a parent who was arguing for the parents' right to choose.

Student civil rights were the subject of the fifth rule. Here there were all kinds of conflicts involving due process and freedom of expression and religion. Students choosing traditional dress, hairstyle, and beliefs were sometimes denied those rights. On the other hand, some tribally controlled schools enforced traditional tribal ways, offending students or parents who did not share that preference.

And last, there was adequate yearly progress (AYP), the requirement in the No Child Left Behind Act that has caused so much stress and resentment across the country. This requirement mandates that every class must demonstrate a certain level of progress every year, measured by student test scores, until 100 percent achievement is attained within a certain number of years. Mainstream schools find it difficult enough to meet the standard, but Indian schools face additional hurdles—lack of proficiency in English, lack of adequate housing and utilities, health problems, and cultural norms that conflict with mainstream learning styles. In addition, the adequate yearly progress standard does not measure, or even acknowledge, progress that students might make outside the tested areas, such as acquisition of cultural knowledge and native language or practice of traditional arts and crafts.

It was a huge assignment by any measure, and it turned out to be a very complex process. We held five meetings between May and September 2003, each three days long to maximize our time together. Each of those meetings involved juggling the concurrent small-group meetings and the plenary sessions, in which advisors and consultants made presentations and draft regulations were considered. And every meeting, held in a different part of the country, had an audience of local tribal representatives, parents, and sometimes students who wanted to oversee the committee's every move. Once during each meeting day, these observers were given time to give their perspective or offer advice to the committee members. At one particularly contentious meeting, a high school student stood up to address the committee. "I have to say," she said with great maturity, "you look like a bunch of kids fighting over a piece of candy." Although much of the advice from the audience members was valuable, their presence probably affected the negotiations in negative ways, preventing committee members from taking risks and perhaps encouraging posturing. We saw the same phenomenon in chapter 8, where the small-engine negotiators were under the scrutiny of industry representatives during every moment of every meeting.

These process mechanics were complex enough, but I was more concerned with the underlying challenges relating to tribal-federal work. Some tribal participants had been very reluctant to join the committee. In addition to their inherent distrust of the federal government, some were wary about joining a process to which they would be bound. There could be serious recriminations back home if the group they participated in reached an agreement that was damaging to the tribe in some way. Even if they did not offer consensus and went on record opposing the agreement, their names would be on that list of committee members and forever they would be associated with that negative outcome. This was one reason why the Española and Pojoaque Valleys Water and Wastewater Steering Committee (chapter 1) never had a formal membership list. In that case, although non-Indian participants regularly suggested forming a regional water authority, a county task force, or some other official body that could receive recognition and funding, the tribal preference was to remain unorganized and informal, working together in creative ways.

Another scenario was that the definition of "consensus"—which for me is synonymous with "unanimity"—would be changed to "a majority."

The tribal minority interest might be trivialized as the group moved forward to reach an "agreement by consensus" without them. The only option would be to file suit or a formal objection, but then again their position could be undercut by the fact that they were participants in the process.

Finally, signing on to negotiate a complex set of regulations with traditional enemies is no fun. For tribal representatives, it takes time away from pressing duties at home, where resources, expertise, and leadership are all in short supply. It brings up painful reminders of the inequities between different populations, geographies, and cultures in this country. You must face those across the table who do not understand your way of life, values, and cultural practices and who may not even be interested.

In spite of these excellent reasons not to join the work group, a number of tribal leaders and school board members, staff, and parents from around the country accepted the invitation. They admitted that it was better to be part of the process than to be left on the outside, reacting to what others had crafted. And besides, I assured them, a negotiated settlement would move forward only if all supported it. They had veto power if they wished to use it. (I had made the same speech to the environmental interests in the previous chapter who feared that because they were in the minority at the table, they would be outvoted.)

My final promise was that the tribal committee members, like everyone at the table, would be treated fairly and with respect. Of all the complexities I was juggling as the process moved forward, this one had priority for me personally because of my background in Indian country and because I knew it was critical to keeping the tribal team at the table.

At the first meeting, I allowed two hours on the agenda for members to introduce themselves, hoping that this would lay the foundation for some degree of trust at the table, as it had with the group in chapter 3 when Thelma's introduction broke down barriers. Each member had about five minutes. As I expected, tribal members took more time, and we spent the morning on introductions. I defended the time overrun, saying that it was important for us to know one another and this was a good chance to practice listening with respect and an open mind, my number one ground rule for the group.

What people said during their introductions was for the most part encouraging. Everyone was making an effort to show commitment and at least a trace of optimism. In general, the federal representatives expressed willingness to pitch in and bring their considerable expertise and resources to bear. And, in general, the tribal side was passionate about improving education for future generations of Indian children and willing to give this process a chance. It seemed there was some agreement on the goal and the importance of the work.

But when it was Linda's turn to introduce herself, she just shook her head, the first of many such shakes. She said that to be perfectly honest, she could not believe that she was sitting at a negotiating table with the US government, but it was her love of her community and her concern about the next generation that brought her here. I wasn't surprised by her hostility. That sentiment was in the room, and it was just as well, I thought, that Linda had expressed it. It gave me an opening to talk about trust. It had to be earned, and we needed to do the best we could to find it together. I scanned the table and saw a variety of reactions. Some of the feds were looking impatient and uncomfortable.

Linda expressed the same distrust and the same pessimism about the process at the next meeting. Whatever the subject, she connected it to abuses visited on Indian people by the federal government. And, not surprisingly, the federal reaction intensified by a few notches. By the third meeting, it was clear that Linda's volcano was near erupting.

We were discussing how the concept for school funding just approved by the committee would be translated into regulatory language. It was not a controversial topic, but Linda was listening to another drummer. Looking down at her folded hands, she took a deep breath. I called on her, but I didn't need to. At that moment, she was in charge.

It was hard for her to believe she was sitting here, she began, looking sadly around the U-shaped configuration of tables at the twenty-one other members of the working group. She was supposed to represent her people in this negotiation with the US government, when history told her this was a very dangerous proposition. She couldn't imagine signing anything at the end of this process, even if the regulations were good ones. I had a flashback to Elaine at the last meeting of the small-engine negotiations (chapter 8), refusing to sign on principle.

I heard a rustling on the other side of the table. Ellen, a federal member, was riffling through her notebook impatiently. She was young and wiry, with short blond hair, and she oozed competence. She could have written these regulations happily by herself, and she seemed already to be regretting the team approach. She was not alone. I scanned the table and saw several distressed faces, both federal and tribal. Linda went on.

"In the 1880s, the winters were really harsh in the Dakotas, and people were starving and sick. The cavalry brought blankets. We took them. We trusted the soldiers. We didn't know any better then." She looked up, straight at the attorney from the Department of the Interior. "Now we know better. Those blankets had smallpox in them, and the soldiers knew it. Hundreds of our people died . . . a terrible death. My great-grandmother told me the story, and I heard about it from others in our community when I was growing up. And I've told it to my children and grandchildren. It was a terrible thing for my people, and it is not over. That's our history with the US government, just a small part of it." She looked down again, and her voice shook. "My family warned me not to join this committee—that it would just lead to more grief, that the government could not be trusted. Sometimes I can't sleep at night. I'm afraid they are right."

She stopped to gather herself, and I quickly looked around the table. I saw a variety of reactions on the non-Indian faces. Ellen shot me a sullen, accusatory look. A young woman was crying; another woman's face was bright red; a man caught my glance and made the sign of "cut her off," drawing his finger across his throat and rolling his eyes. Another man had his elbows on the table, his head in his hands. The tribal members were looking stoic; one was fiddling with a paper clip, and another was staring straight ahead, lips pursed.

A federal attorney who had been looking at Linda intently couldn't remain silent. "It wasn't my ancestors who did those bad things. I'm Irish. My people came to New York during the potato famine. They suffered, they almost died, over there." He paused, wondering whether to go ahead and underline his point. "I mean . . . the truth is . . . other people suffered, too."

A federal teammate chimed in. She was Jewish, and she didn't think it was fair to include her in this mass indictment of white people. After all, Jews had suffered attempted extermination, too. All of this may have made the speakers feel better, but it had no effect on Linda. She sat stone-faced, saying nothing.

Finally, a frustrated federal member let loose: "We have a hell of a lot of work to do, and we don't have time to hear this!"

As facilitator, I was walking a tightrope, trying to be culturally sensitive while managing an equitable and productive process. I needed to honor the voice who wanted to get the work done, but I also needed to validate what Linda was saying. And she was not the only one. There were others during the meetings whose resentment and suspicion broke through as they sent a barb across the table. The Anglo side, generally, was interested in meeting deadlines and delivering a product, and I knew many wanted me to refocus the group and push forward with our work. But if the tribal side was to stay at the table, we needed to take the time necessary to deal with issues of trust. Without that, no agreement would be reached anyway.

That was my thinking from the very beginning, and here we were at the third meeting, with no end in sight to these digressions. I was giving Linda time, but it was not satisfying her. Could this be a power play? After all, each party musters power however he or she can. Lawyers tend to speak legalese and wear fancy suits; scientists come with stacks of data; bureaucrats can raise all kinds of barriers to what seems like a reasonable idea. And for the tribal contingent, playing the "culture" card or the "historical abuse" card is always an option, and an especially attractive one if the facilitator is so inclined. I had no choice but to take Linda at face value. She was in pain, real pain, and I needed to deal with it. I realized that Linda was going to bring this up until she was heard, not just tolerated but really heard. Most of the federal members shut down when she began. I was the only one who gave her any indication that she had been heard and understood.

As Linda wound down, she began to cry. Ellen rolled her eyes. The young woman who had been weeping blew her nose. The red-faced one dug in her purse. Others looked uncomfortable at best. On behalf of the group, I needed to hear Linda.

"I have just realized something," I said to her. "We've been focusing on these regulations that will impact Indian country in the future, but this isn't just about the future. The past is here, too, and you remind us of that. It is with you in everything you do, everywhere you go." I went on and talked briefly about historical trauma, a subject studied by anthropologists and psychologists, but, I acknowledged, for Linda and others it was a part of everyday life. The rest of us might understand intellectually, but we could never feel the personal pain that she was expressing. I tried to offer support for the non-Indians at the table, too, acknowledging that hearing painful history makes us uncomfortable and impatient. "We think it doesn't have anything to do with why we're here and that it is taking valuable time away from our task. But I am guessing that until we all really hear what is being said, until we see that for many here, history is actually part of the present and the future, we will not have enough trust to reach an agreement."

I looked at Linda. She was wiping her nose. Wisps of dark hair straggled from the big beaded barrette at the back of her head. She looked tired and defeated as usual, the creases in her face more pronounced, her shoulders hunched. But her eyes, big and brown, were less tearful, and they looked at me with curiosity. "Am I understanding you, Linda?"

"Yes. History has to be here. We don't have a choice." She gave her nose a final wipe.

I looked around the table. At least I had everyone's attention. I was struggling to express something that was little more than a hunch, a hunch that this topic of history—historical trauma—needed more attention, not less. Without validation, it would keep rising up, demanding acknowledgment and legitimacy. I had an idea that I confessed might be crazy. I suggested that history was so important in this particular group that it deserved its own seat at the table. If I were designing the process again, I would add an extra chair for history so we would understand its significance from the beginning. "But," I added, "maybe it's not too late," and I dragged a chair from against the wall, placing it at the table between Linda and an attorney from the Department of the Interior. They both moved over to make room for the new member. "Now history has a legitimate place at the table. This can be a reminder to all of us." All eyes were on the empty chair.

"We didn't order a box lunch for History." Every group (blessedly) has its joker.

"History is fasting," answered Linda with a faint smile.

I knew I had taken a chance by siding with Linda on the question of history at the table. Most on the federal side had made it clear to me, both publicly and privately, that they were sick of the "whining about the past," and after this meeting they asked to meet with me in caucus. They accused me of being too pro-Indian, which at the time struck me as very funny, given that they were working for the Bureau of Indian Affairs, and I assumed that we were all pro-Indian.

But bias is a very serious accusation for a mediator. We pledge to treat all parties fairly and with respect, and I never doubted my ability to do that. I could see how the federal team could perceive me as being "soft on the Indians," as they said. Would I have allowed a non-Indian to take the stage with a similar diversion? Probably not. Sure sounds like bias. But what about the other obligation of the mediator: to balance power? Maybe my efforts to balance power by validating Linda's historical trauma could be perceived as bias. It was, and remains, a troubling question for me.

I listened respectfully to the federal team and tried to explain my strategy. If the federal members could show that they had really heard these painful stories, I suggested, they might be surprised to see Linda shift her focus to the work at hand. An Anglo school administrator from Arizona said he had learned the same lesson the hard way. But from the others, I had a cold reception. I apologized for any remarks that seemed offensive or biased and urged them to feel free to raise these issues in the group if they felt I was out of line in any way. "Oh, God," muttered Ellen. "That's the last thing I want to do. We'd never get anything done!"

My relationship with some of the federal team members was strained during the rest of the process, but I remained focused on the more fragile and volatile Indian members, who I still feared might resign. The federal representatives had no choice. It was their job to be there. They might want to walk out, but they couldn't.

It turned out that Linda was able to move forward, and she did sign the consensus agreement at the end of the process, although I'm sure with anxiety. With completion of the six regulations, developed by consensus in five months, the Department of the Interior leadership declared the process a great success. Both the substance and the process received an A+ from the client. But how did the participants feel? Did they form relationships? Would they sign up for another, similar process? The experience cannot have been very satisfying for Linda and probably others on the tribal side. And although the federal members had every right to feel proud of their work, several of them said that they would never agree to participate in another FACA committee. It wasn't worth it, they said. It was too hard.

I thought about that. What could be so hard? They weren't the ones with the painful past. Then I realized that to have to sit and hear an eloquent Native woman describe tragic events from the past and their impact on present daily life was very painful for the listeners, especially the white listeners. They may have been looking forward to a new experience, working side by side with Native people. But they were not prepared for the accusations, the attack on their identity, and the onslaught of emotions. With my experience working in Indian country, I had seen the wounds of historical trauma in many tribal people—friends, colleagues, and participants in processes like this one. I had learned the power of listening, taking the pain inside yourself, and making it clear to the teller that you understand, as best an outsider can. But I had forgotten the vulnerability, the deep sadness, the guilt that you can feel as a non-Indian when the past abuse and current suffering are made real by one person's story. I regret not acknowledging that pain as very real for the non-Indians at the table. I could have told them that I knew very well what they were feeling. I had felt it myself many, many times.

I want to give a little equal time to the moments of psychological satisfaction in the No Child Left Behind Act regulatory negotiation and, in the process, introduce you to one of my co-facilitators, Ray Daw. At our first meeting, each small-group facilitator chose a regulation. Ray, a Navajo from New Mexico, had chosen to work with the tribally run school grant regulation, a thorny issue that interested him. The director of a substance abuse treatment center in Gallup, New Mexico, he was trained and experienced in counseling and program management, not in facilitation and mediation. I had a lot of confidence in Ray's engaging, unflappable, and patient way. I knew he would bring both his professional skills as a counselor and his healing skills as a medicine man to the process. But I wanted him to have the least demanding group because he was by far the least experienced facilitator on the team. When the four most aggressive committee members, from both the government and Indian sides, rushed forward to sign up for his work group, I checked with him.

"No problem," he said. "I'll keep 'em in line," and he laughed.

This was on the second day of our first meeting. The previous day, when we all introduced ourselves, Ray had given his name and his clan identification in Navajo and then interpreted for the group. He described his many roles in his community—medicine man, counselor, baseball coach for boys and girls—and explained the cultural and personal importance of relationships, family, and future generations. In his fifties, with long, wispy gray hair in the traditional *bits'iis* (knotted and wrapped with white yarn at the back of his neck), Ray spoke in a soft voice that commanded attention. Generous, open, and good-hearted, he could light up a room with his smile and twinkling gray eyes. When he made a joke—which was often—his laugh was contagious. The way he walked and stood was special and hard to explain. It was as if he were planting himself with every step, as if he could stop at any moment and spend the rest of his life there, perfectly comfortable. I enjoyed seeing the committee members relax within Ray's sphere of influence. He was embracing them without making a move.

Ray had charm and got instant respect from both the federal and tribal sides, but plunging with minimal facilitation experience into one of the funding regulations was another matter. Agreeing on the criteria for allocation of grants and on how to coordinate the various programs with their often conflicting mandates was going to be a challenge. What would he do with this fearsome foursome—two federal lawyers, a school board president, and a tribal leader, all strong personalities that already, in the space of a few hours, had made their very significant needs known? After three hours, I finally had a free moment and headed straight for Ray's group to check in and take over if I needed to.

I opened the door and could not have been more surprised. There they were, all five around a small table, laughing good-naturedly. Ray was at his laptop, with a quiet smile on his face, looking at the screen while the current regulation was projected on the wall. The body language said it all. In the meeting the day before, each group member had been upright, leaning forward, chin jutting out, on the attack. Now they all looked like a group of friends who were watching a movie together. They were lounging in their chairs, facing the projected text on the wall. The lawyer, who had been pounding her fist on her notebook on day one, was leaning back with her feet up on a spare chair. Facing her was the bemused tribal leader with his elbow on the table, his hand propping up his head, while he twirled his pen with the other hand. The other two had their hands clasped behind their heads, legs stretched out in front of them. Piled on the table were yellow pads, open law books, an avalanche of loose papers, and sodas and chips. Their laughter quieted as I entered. They gave me no more than a glance.

"Hi," I said, realizing I sounded like a mother who just can't resist spying on her teenager's slumber party. "How's it going?"

"Good. We're doing pretty good," Ray said with a reassuring smile, and passed the question to the others with a nod.

"No problems here," said the lawyer jauntily.

"Yeah, we're moving right along . . . like a herd of sheep." The school board president had triggered some kind of inside joke. They all laughed.

Ray turned back to his keyboard. "So what about section 143.b? What did we decide about that?" he asked. It could have been the biggest land mine in all the regulations, but he made it sound as if he were asking, "Shall we have butter on our next bucket of popcorn?"

The group members shifted in their chairs, flipped through papers, and went back to work. Feeling like the outsider that I was, I left.

Ray's group finished its task at the next meeting, way ahead of the others. Radiating pride, they brought their product to the full committee for tentative consensus. They added that they thought they had a lot to offer the other work groups, so each of them was going to join one of the other groups.

I asked Ray for his secret. He laughed, eyes twinkling. "I just let them do it. It was pretty easy. I kept track of everything for them on the laptop, and when they saw how easy it was, they turned into missionaries—couldn't wait to help the other groups!"

I knew it couldn't have been that easy to turn adversaries into missionaries. What allowed them to drop all those defenses and work together? It's true that parties usually find it easier to work in a smaller group, away from the eye of observers and the scrutiny of other team members. You can try things out—proposals or different negotiating styles—that you might be reluctant to try in the larger group. Even dedicated enemies can let down their guard if they get out of the limelight. (This is part of what enabled the ranchers and the environmentalists in chapter 7 to come together in their alliance in the Boot Heel of New Mexico.) Another factor may have been a competitiveness in this foursome of type A personalities that drove them to finish their work first, to show that it was no big deal to sit down and hammer out a solution.

But I give a large dose of credit to Ray's personality and style. He was able to walk into that small room with the expectation that all would go smoothly. He brought optimism with him, not the baggage so many of us do. We can't leave behind our anxieties and our biases, and, like dogs, those parties we are mediating will sniff out that expectation and live up to it. I like to watch Cesar Millan, television's Dog Whisperer, who can handle the most obstinate dog and the most dysfunctional owner like a magician. He says the key is a "calm and assertive" attitude. (I confess that I have reminded myself to be "calm and assertive" before entering a room of rabid dogs around the negotiating table, and that to my surprise it seems to work.) I'm sure Ray, like Cesar, has that quiet confidence that calms a group. That, coupled with his ability to envision the best in people, makes him a very special mediator.

The result is a grade of A+ in psychological satisfaction for participants. In that small group relationships were formed, people worked easily and respectfully together, and I'm sure in that moment all four would have signed up for another, similar process . . . at least, if Ray were the facilitator.

CHAPTER TEN

When Cookies Aren't Enough

Imagine there is a toxic waste pile of uranium tailings just a half mile from your house. The waste is leaking into the groundwater and moving in a "plume," as the scientists call it, away from the site and fanning throughout the aquifer. You must haul drinking water from town because the state has condemned your well. Your family had been using that well forever, but one day the authorities suddenly decided that the levels of radium were dangerously high.

The pile of deadly tailings was supposed to be have been sealed permanently, never to be exposed to the air, but now it is covered with a maze of cracks. Plants sprout from the cracks; you and your neighbors wonder if they glow in the dark. You are sure that the laundry you hang out to dry is dusted with the poison. The rate of childhood cancers seems way above normal, and your own child is sick with something the doctors cannot diagnose. You wonder if they just don't want to tell you that it's cancer, if they are protecting the company that did all this to you and your community.

The industry that left this disaster also took your livelihood and your assets with it when it abandoned ship. There are no jobs. You would have to pay someone to take your house off your hands—it is worthless. You are stuck. You cannot leave. What on earth can a "community informational meeting" do for you—besides enrage you further? How dare these government agencies with their acronyms and jargon and fancy technical words come here to deliver more bad news without offering any real help? How about clean drinking water? How about compensation for all that's lost, or at least all that can carry a price tag?

This was the poor soul who would be joining equally desperate neighbors to hear an update on cleanup activities at a Superfund site west of Albuquerque near Grants, New Mexico. My colleague Dexter Albert and I would be facilitating the community meeting for the Environmental Protection Agency (EPA), trying to help achieve some degree of genuine communication that might lead to improved relations. We saw our job as creating a safe environment in which the agency leads could listen to what was being said without becoming defensive and the community members could express themselves honestly without losing control. Our challenge was to gain the trust of the agency lead. If he, like Colonel Mike DeBow (chapter 6), could sit back and let us design the meeting, set the ground rules, and establish a tone of respect and openness, we could open the door to a new kind of relationship in which both agency and community were on the same side. Stacked against us was a legacy of painful meetings, a lack of agency resources to do proper outreach, and a high level of frustration in the community. And, unfortunately, we already knew that our client was no Colonel DeBow.

I love to work with Dexter. He is Navajo, speaks the language fluently, and always brings a calm and a patience to my more frenetic ways. And of course he is a great joker, of the deadpan variety, so I am always on my toes. He is in his late thirties and lives in Flagstaff, where he worked for legal services before hanging out his shingle as a public involvement specialist. He is round faced with a crew cut, stocky, and only a little taller than I am. I always feel as if I have my impish, unpredictable nephew with me when we work together.

The area around the Superfund site is checkerboarded with Indian (Navajo, Acoma, and Laguna) communities interspersed with Anglo ranches and Hispanic villages. Dexter's mother still lives twenty-five miles north of the Superfund site in the traditional Navajo sheep camp where he grew up. Although she was probably far enough from the site to be safe from its toxicity, the family had many relatives and friends who had worked in the mines, who had lost their jobs, and who were beginning to suffer from medical problems. In fact, Dexter and I had teamed up for this job because of his connections and credibility in the area. We looked forward to designing a quality process for the EPA.

But we soon found out that the EPA was just looking for "hired guns" to handle the crowd at the required annual community informational meeting. For the past six years, the agency had sent technical staff to the annual meeting to explain incomprehensible data, which only further frightened and angered those who attended. Trying to defend themselves against the growing anger of the community, the agency staff limited the time each citizen could speak to three minutes. They answered only "clarifying" questions that related to the technical presentation, refusing to respond to any other comments or questions. Needless to say, each year the situation got worse, and knowing that this year would be the most volatile yet, the EPA called for help "to keep control of the situation." In spite of instincts that told us to say no, we were drawn to the challenge and thought we might be able to help, even under these far from ideal conditions.

We pressed for a chance to interview a few community leaders before the meeting. This would give us a better understanding of the landscape—physical, social, and emotional—and we would have a few familiar faces in the audience. Our EPA contact nixed the idea; he had sent out an information sheet a few months earlier and believed that was adequate. We continued to push, even offering to do the interviews at no additional cost, but to no avail. All we were to do was show up on the night of the meeting.

Since the meeting began at 6 p.m. and likely would go past 9 or 10, we asked what kind of refreshments the agency would provide. "No refreshments" was the reply. A federal agency could not provide refreshments for a meeting. It's true that federal law forbids feeding people with federal money, but I have often paid for refreshments myself rather than have an already crabby crowd be hungry as well. We proposed to stop on the way to the meeting and pick up some snacks at our own expense. I would bring my fifty-cup coffeemaker and cups. No, said our agency contact. That would "raise expectations." When we pressed him, he answered that it was just not a good idea, that they had never done it before. We could see the handwriting on the wall. Next year, when the agency was on its own again or with other, more compliant hired guns, they didn't want participants expecting to be fed.

Dexter and I agreed that to go without refreshments was not an option. Coming from Santa Fe, I stopped on my way into town and picked up cookies and fruit. Dexter, coming from Flagstaff, stopped for lemonade and iced tea. At 5 p.m. we met, defiantly, shopping bags in hand, on the steps of city hall and went inside. We left our supplies in the hallway and went to check out the meeting room, the Grants City Council chambers. I have learned the hard way to arrive early and make sure the room is going to work. There are so many things that can go wrong, from microphones and PowerPoint presentations—in fact, those problems are guaranteed—to locked restrooms, no heat, or a basketball tournament under way.

We were relieved to see that everything seemed in order. In fact, a man was setting up folding chairs in a neat arch pattern facing the front of the chambers. Wanting to thank the maintenance person for setting up the chairs, we approached him, smiling.

"Thanks for setting up the chairs. Can we give you a hand?" I said.

"Oh, no. I'm doing fine. Thanks anyway. Are you Lucy?" I was more than surprised that the maintenance man would know my name, and then I realized that this must be someone from the EPA. And on closer examination I saw that he looked much more like a bureaucrat nearing retirement than a janitor. I introduced Dexter, and we all shook hands.

It turned out that he was the EPA community liaison for the site, but he lived in Dallas and spent very little time in the area. He was a senior volunteer employee for the agency—a retired high school history teacher—and seemed to be enjoying this change of pace and subject matter. We asked him for advice about the upcoming meeting, and he laughed, saying that we probably knew more than he did. When we asked if he would like to make any welcoming remarks or be recognized at the start of the meeting, he blanched. "No, no, I'll be sitting in the back, but thanks anyway. Just glad you're here," he added, smiling. "We certainly needed some help last time," he commented and then turned back to his chair arranging.

Dexter and I were discouraged by the encounter. This seemed like another lost opportunity for the agency. The community liaison could be a valuable presence on the ground, keeping lines of communication open between residents and the agency, interpreting new data, and passing on local questions and concerns to the regional office. Using a retired volunteer for this role could be a result of shrinking budgets for EPA work, or it could be another symptom of what I realized was a quite natural fear of getting too close to the community. Or it could be both. The truth was that no one wanted to be at the meeting, not the community members and not the agency representatives. For the residents, it was torture to listen year after year to these technical talking heads. The bureaucrats seemed to evade the real problems, hiding behind jargon, numbers, projections, and impossible scientific words. Then they packed up their laptops, collected their technical reports and handouts, and left in their government vans.

But for the agency folks it was torture, too. (Again, I was reminded of the Bureau of Indian Affairs staff in chapter 9, who were accountable to the Indian population they served but were often seen as the enemy.) They in no way had caused the terrible toxic situation that had trapped these people; in fact, they were actually on their side, trying to clean things up. But with the mining companies long gone, the agencies were faced with angry people in pain who blamed them for everything. There was little the bureaucrats and scientists could do for these people. There wasn't enough money, and in one of the poorest areas of one of the poorest states, this site had no clout. The community liaison / retired history teacher had no desire to spend any more time than he had to with these people. Getting to know them would only increase his discomfort. His inability to improve their lives would only fill him with guilt. The sad thing was that this culture of avoidance, very understandable from a human perspective, added fuel to the fury of those suffering residents. In my opinion, a little compassion, a little time spent with them, might do some good.

And maybe a cookie could help, too. Dexter and I returned to our table of refreshments. He opened the lemonade and iced tea while I filled the coffeemaker in the restroom sink. I dripped my way back to the refreshment table, dumped in the grounds, and plugged it in. It was a very familiar ritual for me and one I liked. It gave me the illusion of having neighbors over for a chat . . . although, of course, I knew better.

As we were finishing up, a van from the New Mexico Environment

Department pulled up. Several young technical staff members got out, armed with projector and screen, laptops, and miles of extension cord. They were friendly and seemed inordinately glad to see us. "It was really bad last time," a young woman said after introducing herself as the state hydrologist. "Really bad."

"Like how bad? In what way?" I asked.

"They were so upset, the community. They were really angry." She paused. "I don't blame them. It's a terrible situation." She went on to explain that the mining company had kept its promise to provide clean drinking water to the community for ten years, on the assumption that cleanup would be complete by then. Water deliveries had stopped at the ten-year mark, but the site was far from clean. In fact, the plume of contamination was migrating toward new populations. The company had gone bankrupt, leaving the mess in the hands of the feds and the state. The state had been bringing drinking water to some residents, she explained, but now there were no more funds to continue that program. She feared this was going to be the last straw.

She and her colleagues moved on into the council chambers to set up their equipment. Dexter and I looked at each other briefly and went back to arranging the cookies and fruit on plastic plates—deck chairs on the Titanic, I thought to myself.

The EPA staff arrived next, carrying boxes of handouts. We introduced ourselves, having only talked to our Dallas contact on the phone. He eyed the refreshments.

"Oh, you got refreshments after all." He looked worried.

I answered cheerily, repeating our rationale that people would be hungry, given the meeting's hours. He shrugged and walked away.

My frustration was mounting. Our contract included the words "facilitate dialogue between the community and the agencies," but how could that happen when we were thwarted at every turn? In the end, I feared that we would simply facilitate the handing out of piles of paper and the presentation of confounding data. If I couldn't make it better for these people—give them clean water, make their children well, compensate them for the loss of property—I at least wanted to have an honest, respectful exchange, and in my mind that included cookies.

People began to arrive. Dexter and I split up to chat with the early birds. It was a principle of mine to arrive early enough to greet the first arrival and get acquainted if possible. It gave me comfort to know someone in the audience, even if ever so briefly and superficially. Later, when the going got rough, I could look at the person and think, "Well, at least I have one friend out there." I approached a man who was seated in the front row. That in itself is noteworthy, since 99 percent of meeting goers shun the front row and pile into the back seats, even dragging more chairs to create more back rows. And then without exception someone in the last row will shout "Can't hear!" or "Can't see the screen from here." If I point out an entire row right in front vacant, waiting for them, they frown and root themselves deeper into their last-row seat. But here was one in a hundred, someone who chose the front row. Curious, I approached and introduced myself. He mumbled, "Pleased to meet ya."

"I'm hoping there will be a good turnout tonight," I said, the equivalent of weather talk for a facilitator.

"Oh, there'll be a lot folks here tonight. Guarantee it."

"Was there publicity?" This was another battle that Dexter and I had with the client. We had suggested radio spots and an article in the newspaper. The response was that the agency always ran an announcement in the legal section, and they saw no reason to spend extra money on advertising. "Nope. Never is. But we keep an eye out for that small print. We knew they were coming sometime around now."

I laughed. "Good for you. That's being a sharp citizen! I know that sometimes the agency doesn't make it easy . . ."

He looked at me for the first time. "Who do you work for?"

"I'm a facilitator. I work for all kinds of agencies and private groups. This time, the EPA is paying my bill, but I will be working for everyone who will be in the room tonight." It was a common question and a standard answer.

He gave a slight sound of understanding and looked away.

"You know you're one in a hundred in my experience, sitting in the front row by choice."

"Got a hearing problem . . . and well, I don't see so good either," he said, smiling. "I don't want to miss anything."

We chatted. He was a retired uranium miner living a few miles from the Superfund site. His son and family lived closer to the site, and one of his grandsons had died two years ago of bone cancer at the age of eight. Another child was always sick with one thing or another. They couldn't figure out what was wrong, but Grandpa suspected the tailings pile. He himself had developed kidney cancer at forty-eight, but they had caught it in time, and for the past twelve years he had been all right. It was hard to hear his story. I teared up when he told me about his grandsons. I told him I had grandsons, too, and couldn't imagine the unthinkable. He appreciated that and held onto my hand for an extra beat when I stood up to leave.

Dexter and I spent the next few minutes going over the agenda with the staff members from the four agencies there to present information. This year, the EPA and the State of New Mexico were joined by the federal Agency for Toxic Substances and Disease Registry and the Nuclear Regulatory Commission, both with more inscrutable acronyms and jargon. We wanted to give them all the support we could, knowing that the more open, honest, and human they could be, the more chance there would be of a productive, civil meeting. We asked the presenters to be clear, to avoid using acronyms and explain the technical terms, and to be patient with the questioners. We all knew that an audience member was likely to disguise a rant in the form of an unanswerable question. We assured them we would handle that for them. We suggested that agency staff listen, really listen, to what the audience said. As I had told Colonel DeBow and his crew as they prepared for the community meetings around Abiquiu Reservoir (chapter 6), what they heard might be inaccurate, unfair, or painful, but respectful listening was the only way to begin to build trust with the residents. And if they could reflect what they heard to the speaker, that would be even better. Most looked skeptical. I knew that our only hope was to model that approach ourselves and hope that it would give them courage. When I said that we would not put time limits on audience participation but would take responsibility for moving people along, our EPA contact looked at us as if we were traitors. Now I was positive we would never work on this site again.

It was close to 6 p.m. and the chairs were nearly filled, from the back row forward. My new friend was still the only one in the front row. I smiled at him as Dexter and I walked to the front of the room. He made a tip-of-the-hat sign to me. The murmuring conversations began to wind down. This was always when I was most nervous. Once we began, I would be busy listening, taking notes, making eye contact, monitoring the room, and empathizing. There would be no time for nervousness then. I leaned toward Dexter and whispered in his ear, "Do you want to start, or do you want me to start?" One of us would facilitate and the other would take the flip chart notes, and then we would trade off. I always liked to begin, to make that initial contact with the audience, establish myself with them. But I had many more years' experience, and as a mentor to Dexter, I let him choose.

Without hesitation, he said, "I'll start."

"Good," I said, lying. "I'll be ready to trade whenever you want." I moved in back of him and took my place at the flip chart.

I imagined he was nervous, too, and wondered how he felt being Navajo in front of a crowd of very hurt and angry non-Indians. We had expected a good number of Navajos in the audience, but our contact explained that although there were Navajo communities scattered in the area, they were under the jurisdiction of the San Francisco EPA region, not the Dallas region, and therefore would not be invited. We protested and lost again.

Dexter called the group to order and welcomed them to the agencies' community informational meeting. He introduced himself, including his clan membership, and then asked agency staff members to give their names and positions. They were seated in a small choir section to our far left.

Dexter continued with explanations of the agenda and the handout materials, a nod to the maps and time lines on the wall, and an invitation to partake of the refreshments in the hall. Dexter was doing fine, and I had nothing to worry about. But I was curious about the folder that he held open in one arm, like a songbook, and glanced at occasionally. I didn't remember seeing him take notes before we started, but he must have. That was smart of him, I thought. I moved up beside and behind him casually, not distractingly, I hoped, and peeked over his shoulder at the folder. On one side was a blank yellow pad. Not a word on it. On the other side was a large color photo of his two daughters, ages eleven and six. They were what he was looking at. They were his notes, his agenda, his mission. I turned back to the flip chart, my eyes tearing up for the second time that evening—already.

The meeting began with a series of presentations of the latest scientific findings relating to contamination at the site. First was a summary of the EPA's groundwater optimization study, scheduled to be released in the next month or two. I had a hard time understanding what an optimization study was, but it seemed to be an effort to evaluate how well the current remediation was addressing community requests. Next, the state described a project to test wells uphill (in groundwater terms) from the Superfund site, including in a small village. Villagers had requested the study last year, and the results, they were told, should be public a year from now.

Finally, the Nuclear Regulatory Commission staff updated the group on several activities designed to address contamination. These included revising the Corrective Action Plan, conducting air-monitoring projects, monitoring the journey of the contamination plume in the groundwater, licensing amendments for an evaporation pond, and drawing up plans for more evaporation ponds. These ponds, part of the cleanup strategy, would receive contaminated water pumped from the aquifer; after evaporation, the contaminants would be captured and safely contained somewhere. One problem already identified was the white residue left by the spraying mechanisms. Just what was it, and how far was it traveling?

I felt for the agency representatives. Every remediation effort seemed to bring with it more problems. In the privacy of their offices and labs they must have been frustrated, wishing for a solution that would truly remedy all the woes at the site. It was all so complicated; how on earth could they explain it to a layperson, especially a layperson unable to hear anything through the pain of his or her particular situation? I could barely follow the presentations myself.

Audience members interrupted frequently to ask questions and sometimes to make a speech. Dexter did his best to keep the presentations on track, assuring everyone that the meeting would last as long as there were still questions. After the presentations, we opened the floor for the residents to speak. Their comments fell in two categories: the contamination (past, present, future) and the communication between agencies and the community.

Many people were worried about the movement of the plume of contamination toward the town's water supply and asked for testing of the migration more often than the standard two or three years. There was also concern that the agencies were pumping clean water into the contaminated aquifers in an effort to dilute the pollution. The solution to pollution is not dilution, said a resident.

Others were bitter that the mining company, now defunct, was no longer providing them with clean drinking water. "The state came out, tested wells, and told us the water wasn't safe to drink," said a resident, "and we never saw you again." There was confusion and suspicion because one resident seemed still to be receiving drinking water, but here the agency was tongue-tied, prohibited by law to discuss individual private wells in a public setting. The state hydrologist with whom I had talked as she was unloading the van offered to talk privately with anyone whose well had been closed and who needed bottled water. She also promised to see if annual testing of the town's supplies would be possible. Clearly, she was in a no-win position and doing the best she could.

Many during the evening urged the agencies to look at the whole picture of contamination rather than dividing the affected region into so many different sites. Residents were frustrated by having to deal with multiple sites, agencies, regulations, schedules, and personalities depending on the location of the problem, the source and type of contamination, and whether it impacted air, soil, groundwater, or surface water. They asked for a comprehensive, complete, coordinated study of the area's contamination and a single overarching Superfund site. As for the cleanup under way, people wondered whether the standards were high enough. The agency representatives explained that the cleanup standards must be based on background levels—the amounts of various contaminants that occurred naturally in the region. They could not spend tax dollars making the air, the water, or the soil cleaner than it was before the mining began. Obviously, this area was rich in uranium and other potentially toxic materials; that's what made it attractive to mining companies. But with no data about the levels of these naturally occurring substances, the agencies were guessing on the basis of levels in similar regions, a methodology the audience thought unfair.

The slow pace of cleanup was another frustration. The contamination from the site had spread to 5,000 acres and five aquifers. "Two years ago—hell, ten years ago—we were talking about exactly the same things," said one. A resident acknowledged that the agencies seemed to be trying to make progress, but too often it looked as if they were "dragging their feet." When asked for a deadline for the completed cleanup, the agency representatives were silent, afraid to make a prediction.

There were dozens of other topics people wanted to talk about. Some were sophisticated questions about water-sampling methodology and the plan for closing abandoned wells. Others were anecdotal. Buildings in the area were suffering structural damage. Could it be from the extraction and injection activities in the aquifer? There were plants peeking through the cover of the tailings piles. Doesn't this mean that contaminants could be escaping through those breaks?

And of course there were stories about health: loss of loved ones, unexplained illnesses, seemingly high rates of cancer. Could somebody come and give physical exams and do testing? And what about property values? One resident said that, unable to sell their homes at any price, they were "trapped in a nightmare, stuck here being poisoned, unable to leave."

There is always someone—usually just one—in a crowd like this who is able to take a longer view in spite of being intimately involved with the problem. I marvel at such people. This audience member observed toward the end of the meeting that it is hard to answer tough questions in hindsight. Regulations, knowledge, and awareness were different when the mining began, he said. "We didn't know what we should ask and what we should look for back then. Now we know better." His neighbors listened to him with respect; no one refuted or added to his point. Agency staff, by now exhausted, looked at him with curiosity, as if they might be hearing things.

There were questions about communication and coordination, both internally among the four agencies and between the agencies and the community. Residents were overwhelmed by the avalanche of data they were expected to download (a challenge for many in itself) and understand. They weren't professionals, they said. No one was going to pay them to become the experts they needed to be. I had heard this complaint often from members of the public trying to master technical information. Not being able to access information or understand it "adds to the perception that the agencies and the company have been engaged in a legacy of deception," suggested a resident. She asked the agencies for help in evaluating the data. An EPA official who had been listening sympathetically volunteered to see if technical assistance could be found to help the community deal with this flood of information. Perhaps it could all be collected at a single Web site, he added, or even as hard copies at the local public library. People were heartened by this offer of real help.

Toward the end of the meeting, some citizens began to soften their tone. They suggested that with their local expertise and experience they could be useful partners to the agencies. A man had aerial photos showing irrigated lands in the 1930s. Would that help establish some kind of baseline for what it was like in the past? Another dragged two big file boxes to the front of the room and said that they were full of papers left behind by Homestake Mining Company. He had found them in an abandoned office building, and he offered them to the agencies.

Citizens asked to be consulted before decisions were made about the cleanup. They knew they didn't have the technical expertise, but still, with the biggest stake in the outcome, they wanted to be part of the decision-making process. At least a few were beginning to see themselves as partners, not just victims, and they were asking the agencies to see them that way, too.

As the meeting was winding down, I was surprised to see a hand go up from the agency choir section to my left. It was the deputy to the deputy EPA regional administrator, the highest-ranking EPA official present. He thanked the participants for their attendance and said that he had learned a lot, that it had been a valuable meeting. Like Colonel DeBow, he had listened to every word. He spoke slowly and thoughtfully, saying he wished he could grant all the requests he had heard, but of course he was limited by budgets and time lines and other factors. He had, however, heard a theme throughout the evening that he wanted to respond to. That was the chronic lack of coordination and communication among the four agencies. He acknowledged that the four presentations of data and plans had been somewhat disjointed and confusing. This he pledged to do something about.

In closing, he said, "I will personally take responsibility for coordinating these four agencies so that our relationship with you, the community, is more productive." There was spontaneous applause from the audience.

It was kind of amazing. This man had not promised to restore health, clean the groundwater, purify the air, or raise property values. He had listened to three hours of testimony from the community and had found something he could respond to, something he could do something about. The residents knew he could only do so much, and they appreciated this step in the right direction.

Dexter and I were ready to close the meeting when one especially hostile citizen thrust up his hand. My heart sank. Here we were ending on a positive note, and this guy was going to get in the last angry word. He stood up. "I'm still damned angry, and you all know it. But this meeting was better than last year, by a long shot. That's all I've got to say." There was a round of applause, and the meeting was over. The presenters were gathering up their equipment, rewinding cords, slipping laptops into cases, boxing up extra materials. Audience members were mingling. Some were talking to agency staff, exchanging cards or phone numbers. Dexter and I folded up the flip chart stand, rolled up the sheets of notes, and headed for the hall to deal with the leftover snacks. My friend from the front row intercepted us.

"You folks did a good job. Didn't let them get away with anything. They listened to us this time. I just wanted to say thank you."

We thanked him for being there and said we hoped to see him next time, although we knew that for us there would be no next time with this client. We had broken the rules. We had raised expectations that the agencies would listen and respond and treat the citizens with the respect and understanding that stakeholders deserve. I wish we had been able to convince the client that this was actually an easier way to relate to the community, that three-minute limits on those who want to speak, stony faces, complex presentations, and no responses were harder on everyone. But try as we did in our final report to make these points, the next year came and went, and the next, without a call.

We weren't surprised. After all, we had broken another rule. We had brought cookies.

CHAPTER ELEVEN

Tribes Take the Lead

Sometimes a case comes along that just has your name written all over it. That's how I felt when the US Department of the Interior (DOI) put out a solicitation for the development of its national tribal consultation policy. The Secretary of the Interior had formed a committee of federal and tribal representatives to negotiate the policy, and my job would be to manage the process—set agendas, establish protocols, facilitate meetings, mediate any conflicts, produce written summaries of the discussions, and generally shepherd the development of the policy.

Having worked in Indian country for decades, I knew how complex and confusing the relationship between tribes and federal agencies could be. In spite of good intentions, not to mention laws and treaties, the mutually respectful partnership contemplated rarely happens. There are so many hazards along the way—inadequate funds, a difficult personality (or two), the legacy of history, competing priorities, and lack of political will, to name only a few. This new, overarching tribal consultation policy would clarify the requirements for the department as well as the role of the tribes, and I was going to be there for the birth.

The federal-tribal relationship is based on a body of treaties, laws, court decisions, and executive orders and their interpretations. What is critical to tribal leaders, and what they want the non-Indian to understand, is that there are two fundamental principles underlying their relationship with the federal government. These are the federal trust responsibility and the government-to-government relationship. Equally important to tribal governments, the two mandates can seem contradictory, or at least ironic, to some.

The trust responsibility requires the federal government, as a whole and in all its parts, to protect the welfare of tribal people and their resources. The federal Bureau of Indian Affairs, housed in the DOI, is now a primary vehicle for the implementation of this responsibility, although most other agencies within the department (as well as in other federal departments, such as Education, Health and Human Services, Energy, and Labor) include policies and programs designed to meet the mandate. This is the basis for the Indian Health Service, Indian education initiatives, housing and roads programs, and many more efforts targeted at a population that was decimated in the early days of this country and today is at or near the bottom in almost all measures of health and success.

The government-to-government relationship embodies the concept that tribal governments are sovereign nations and that, as such, they deserve treatment that is respectful of both tribal rights and culture. Some go so far as to say that tribal governments should have the same status as foreign nations, with currency, passports, embassies, alliances, and modern treaties. Given the reality of current tribal capacities and the intricate weaving of tribal life into mainstream America, this is neither possible nor, for most, desirable, but it underscores the deep belief in the sovereignty of Indian governments. One of the most important expressions of the government-to-government relationship today is found in the practice of tribal consultation.

Tribal consultation, mandated by executive orders and department policies, requires that any federal agency "consult" with a tribal government when a proposed action, regulation, or policy might have an impact on that government, its people, or its resources. The intent is that appropriately high-level representatives of the federal and tribal governments will sit down and discuss the proposal, agreeing on ways that implementation can benefit, or at least do as little harm as possible to, the tribal community. Too often and for too long, this obligation has been inadequately met by agencies going through minimal motions. Typically, a "Dear Tribal Leader letter" is sent by agency staff either unable or unwilling to determine the appropriate name and title of the recipient. So, instead of "Dear Governor Cooeyate," or "Dear President Zah," the letters go out with the salutation "Dear Tribal Leader." I have heard from tribal secretaries that letters such as these, addressed generically, are routinely tossed out or at best go to the bottom of the heap. If opened, they may be sent down a tortuous path from one administrative assistant or department head to another before landing on the right desk. In any case, the federal sender of the letter typically waits a few days, maybe weeks, and then "checks the box," indicating that tribal consultation is complete, even if no contact has been made.

But President Barack Obama would not tolerate a check-the-box policy for tribal matters. He issued a presidential memorandum in November 2009 mandating all federal agencies to plan for and implement meaningful and effective tribal consultation. Executive Order 13175, issued by President Bill Clinton in 2000, had called for improved consultation practices, but in the interim there had been little progress. All department secretaries and agency leads were told to make this a top priority, and Secretary of the Interior Ken Salazar took special notice.

The federal department with the most connections to Indian country is the Department of the Interior. It includes the National Park Service and the Bureau of Land Management, whose lands are often contiguous with tribal lands or in some cases even overlapping; the US Fish and Wildlife Service, whose decisions about endangered species can be good or bad news for tribes; the Bureau of Reclamation, whose water projects can bring water to, or take water from, irrigated Indian land; the US Geological Survey, whose research, data gathering, and labeling can affect tribes; and, of course, the Bureau of Indian Affairs, whose every move is of consequence to tribal members and their governing bodies.

Although all the bureaus and offices of the Department of the Interior had tribal consultation policies in various states of effectiveness or disrepair, Salazar decided that this was a good opportunity to create an overarching policy for the department as a whole. The individual bureaus and offices could retain their policies as long as they conformed to the new department-wide policy, or they could develop new policies tailored to their particular needs as long as they met the new standards.

The challenge was to craft a policy that would uphold the trust responsibility and the government-to-government relationship while guiding bureaucrats in a process that would be implementable and enforceable. The most lofty policy would be useless if those responsible for making it a reality were unable or unwilling to do so. The policy needed to be flexible in order to cover the great variety of situations and players but tight enough to prevent bureaucrats from wiggling out of responsibilities. Just what "consultation" meant was at the heart of the task.

The Secretary of the Interior knew that this would be a high-profile undertaking and that his department could serve as a model—or a warning—for other agencies as they tackled Obama's directive. Further, he knew that tribes would be scrutinizing every move made in the drafting of this new consultation policy. What a perfect opportunity, he thought, to include tribal voices in the actual development of the policy. As did the EPA leadership in chapter 8, he rejected the traditional policy-drafting process that locked his solicitors behind closed doors and instead chose to "set" a policy-drafting table that would include those very interest groups who would have the most to lose or gain. The department's tribal consultation policy would be the result of a true collaboration—the word of the day—between a federal agency and tribes.

Following a series of listening sessions (another word du jour) in Indian country, the department drafted recommendations about how the Secretary should proceed. There would be a committee of tribal leaders (one from each of the twelve BIA regions throughout the country) and federal leaders (one from each of the thirteen bureaus and offices within the department). Each of these twenty-five members would have an alternate, so the total membership would be fifty. The group's charge would be to draft a policy, or perhaps a set of concepts for the policy, that would be delivered to the DOI's Office of the Solicitor to be reviewed for legal or implementation problems. Basically, Salazar was delegating the task of creating the tribal consultation policy to this group, if the members could reach consensus.

For me, this was a very exciting prospect. I had seen federal agencies consult responsibly, and I also had seen them check the box, thanking their lucky stars they didn't have to deal with those Indians. To me, consultation was a critical part of the federal-tribal relationship, and a great concept, but the confusion, frustration, and fear surrounding the consultation requirement meant that it was rarely carried out in a meaningful way—just as Obama said. To help guide the creation of a policy that was clear, implementable, and respectful would be incredibly rewarding for me personally and professionally.

The mediation bible tells us that the first meeting of a negotiating group is crucial for many reasons: the group must agree on a set of protocols or ground rules to govern how it will operate; relationships are formed; and the mediator establishes his or her role and is accepted by the group (one hopes). Negotiating the protocols will be the group members' test run on reaching consensus, and the experience can give a group hope that it will be able to tackle successfully the substantive issues that lie ahead. In some cases, a newly formed group will take two or even three meetings to get through the protocols as the members spar with one another and jockey for position. Sometimes the simplest ground rules—no cell phones, no smoking, no interrupting—can be debated endlessly if the group is in a particular mood. The following are more complex questions facing the group at that first meeting:

- How will the group make decisions? If by consensus, what do group members mean by "consensus"? Will there be majority and minority reports?
- What will be the role of alternates? Should they come to all the meetings? Will they have a "vote"?
- What kind of record keeping does the group want? Will records be made public? Will audio or video recording be allowed?
- How should the press be handled? Does the group want to assign a spokesperson?
- Can members seek alternative avenues for satisfaction during this process—such as going to court, to Congress, to the media?
- How can members be held accountable? How can members be replaced?
- Can the members promise to keep their discussions confidential?
- What kind of authority will the members have to speak for, and decide for, their organization, agency, or government?
- What responsibility will the members have to their governing bodies and their constituents to keep them informed and part of the process?

- What will be the roles of the mediator, the members, and agency staff?
- Will there be subcommittees?

You know by now that I am on the flexible and informal end of the mediator's spectrum. I am considered by some to be undisciplined, unpredictable, and intuitive to a fault. I have colleagues who would double the list of protocol items above. But my experience with the EPA's small-engine committee (chapter 8) and the BIA's schools committee (chapter 9), as well as dozens of other cases, has impressed on me the importance of this first organizational meeting. The questions above, and any others the group wants to raise, must be answered before the group launches into the substance of the conflict. That is my belief, or at least it was.

The organizational meeting of the Department of the Interior's Tribal Consultation Team (DOI-TCT) took place at the Indian Pueblo Cultural Center in Albuquerque in July 2010. My colleague Jon Townsend and I were nervous. We knew that bringing together federal staff and tribal leadership was potentially explosive and that it was impossible to predict what might trigger that explosion. It could be something seemingly trivial, such as the seating arrangement. Should we go with a hollow square, the most equitable configuration? It would have to be very big to hold all fifty people—not practical. Should we put the twenty-five members at a more reasonably sized hollow square and the alternates around the sides of the room? Should we set the room up with "rounds," as they say in the meeting-planning world, putting the participants at round tables scattered through the room? Should we assign seats with name tents to mix the feds and the tribes, or to keep them separate, or should we let people sit where they choose? We knew there should be an opening prayer, but who should offer it—someone from New Mexico, since that was our location? Or some distinguished leader from elsewhere? And what about the agenda? We needed to demonstrate our ability to be both flexible and efficient in managing the meeting. Should we assign times to the various agenda items, knowing that those times would slip, or should we have no times assigned, knowing that a hand would shoot up, before we even began, asking why there were no times on the agenda? The more experience we had, the more potential pitfalls we saw. We made the necessary decisions and hoped for the best.

The agenda made it clear that the purpose of the two-day meeting was to agree on the DOI-TCT operating procedures and to begin to develop some working relationships. Jon volunteered to handle the introductory section, including a warm-up exercise. I often feel awkward about the icebreaker phase of an agenda. It is hard to read the willingness of a new group to participate in something that might be considered frivolous; sometimes it is just what is needed, and sometimes it backfires and the mediator is left holding a bag of tricks and feeling foolish. Jon had an easy confidence about this early stage, and I was happy to let him take the lead. I would take over when it came time to talk about the protocols, and from then on we would share the load as we moved through the two days.

Governor Norman Cooeyate of the Pueblo of Zuni offered the opening prayer, and the highest-ranking DOI representative, a policy advisor to the Assistant Secretary for Indian Affairs, offered some welcoming remarks. Jon's icebreaker went well. We were encouraged by the committee members' willingness to break into groups, learn about one another and find what they had in common, give their group a catchy name, and then present their expectations for the day to the rest of the groups. There was laughter and a good spirit. The expectations were understandably a little guarded, but on the whole group members were hopeful that this was a worthwhile endeavor. Developing a tribal consultation policy for the Department of the Interior was extremely important, they said, and both tribal and federal team members knew they were lucky to be at the table as part of this historic moment.

By the time each group had reported and we had reviewed the agenda and meeting materials, it was time for lunch. I ate in the meeting room, huddled over my notes about protocols. I wanted to present the topic in a way that emphasized its importance as the foundation for the work ahead, but I also realized there was a danger of bogging down in too much process. Groups were usually eager to get to work and often balked at having to talk about the process. I was ready to facilitate a "protocols lite" discussion if need be.

Back from lunch, everyone settled into their seats at the round tables. We had let them sit where they wished, and some tables were mixed federal and tribal, but most were segregated. I scanned the group and launched the subject of protocols, sending it out on what I hoped would be a calm, receptive sea. It was important, I explained, for a group to agree on how the members are going to work together before they undertake the task before them. I told them I had seen a squabble over the definition of "consensus" sink a process at the very point when consensus was being sought on a final agreement. Or, I warned, a fragile trust can be destroyed when one party files suit or goes to the press in the middle of negotiations. These kinds of issues needed to be dealt with up front, and I was ready to guide the committee members. It was a speech I had given often, and I tried to make it engaging, especially because of the potential for an after-lunch slump. I needn't have worried about that.

About fifteen minutes into my remarks, Brian Patterson, tribal leader from United South and Eastern Tribes, stood up and announced a tribal caucus. Although I always invite participants to ask for a caucus whenever they need it, I am rarely stopped midsentence by the request. Brian invited all the tribal leaders to follow him to a room down the hall. He added that talking about protocols was not what he had come for and that he considered it a waste of time. Caught off guard, I protested politely that at least it would be important to decide how members wanted to make decisions and what they meant by "consensus."

"We know all that," he said, and then he turned and left the room. Like ducklings, the tribal members and their alternates followed him through the door. Jon and I quickly compared notes and decided that he should offer to help the tribal caucus and at least find out how long they thought they might be. He left and came back immediately. They did not need help, and they did not know how long they would be. We asked the federal representatives if they would like to caucus, but they were not interested. They turned to the coffeemaker and stale doughnuts from the morning and to their BlackBerrys and cell phones. Naturally confused and concerned, and perhaps insulted, some muttered about getting earlier flights back to Washington, DC, assuming the process was over before it had begun. But I was impressed with their professionalism and their patience as they waited for the tribal leaders to return. Jon and I tried to figure out how to adjust our agenda, but not knowing what was going to come next, we gave up.

After two hours, the tribes returned. With the undivided attention of everyone in the room, Brian spoke for the caucus. There were three points, he said, that would condition their participation in this process.

First, they wanted the federal team to know that the tribal representatives were extremely disappointed, even insulted, that a higher-level DOI representative was not present to launch the process. The tribal leaders present were all presidents, chairs, governors, or high office holders for their tribes. They understood that President Obama could not attend, but they had hoped for someone from Secretary Salazar's office or at least the Assistant Secretary for Indian Affairs. They meant this, Brian said, as no criticism of the federal representatives who were present; they were sure they were highly skilled and would have much to offer the process.

Second, they did not want to talk about protocols. They were extremely busy leaders with pressing issues back home, and they did not come to this two-day meeting to talk about process. They were ready to begin discussing the nature of tribal consultation and the elements of a good policy. They would not tolerate any more talk of ground rules. Period.

Third, they had decided that it would be most appropriate for the tribes to take the lead in drafting the policy. After all, said Brian, who knows better than the tribes what genuine, effective, respectful consultation should look like? The tribal representatives would produce an initial draft policy, they hoped in the next month or two. When they were ready, they would offer it to the federal representatives for their "comments." He said this word with the loaded meaning known so well to those who work in consultation. The federal agency routinely asks the tribe for its "comments," with the promise that they will be "taken into consideration." Brian was not the only one enjoying that turning-of-the-table moment. I saw smiles and nods of understanding from some on the federal side.

Of course, the tribes knew that this would be the DOI's policy and that they would have to negotiate with the federal team for a final product. And even then, the policy would have to go through the legal hoops and the scrutiny of the Office of Management and Budget before it became official. Brian explained that the tribes were still committed to working in partnership with the federal agencies and, in fact, looked forward to a good, productive relationship. Again, appreciation was expressed for the federal team members and their future contribution to the process. For now, the task was in tribal hands. Brian paused. Were there any questions? Jon and I knew we were no longer in control and stood to the side.

I was curious, and a little anxious, about the federal response. There was reason for them to be at least irritated and at most angry. But I needn't have worried. There was an appropriately long silence while people seemed to absorb what had been said, and then someone spoke up.

"We were prepared to go to work on this, and now that . . . well, if you're taking the lead . . . I mean, I'm not sure what we are supposed to be doing, on the federal side."

"You can just sit back and relax until we give you the first draft," offered a tribal member. There was some laughter about how that would never happen with the crush of work bearing down on federal employees.

Another federal member suggested that maybe the Office of the Solicitor could do some work to support the tribal effort, research legal issues, analyze existing policies from other departments for possible concepts and language, and so on. The answer was basically "If you want to, go ahead, but we will be working on our own until we are ready to share what we have."

I couldn't resist defending the much-maligned protocols. "I understand that you don't want to spend time on the protocols," I tentatively ventured. "In fact, at this point I am afraid to even mention the 'P' word"—Brian took a gruff posture, mostly in jest—"but it is important that you all at least decide how you are going to make decisions and what you mean by consensus. It can be unanimous, or it can be a supermajority, or—"

"Tribal people operate by consensus all the time. We know what we mean, and we don't have to talk about it. We live by it. No more about ground rules." Brian looked around and got nods from his team members. The feds looked at me with compassion but remained silent. I retreated, and Brian and his colleagues led the group in a discussion of good principles of consultation and possible frameworks for the new policy. He asked me and Jon to take notes.

Whatever discomfort surrounded the tribal takeover was much diminished by the next day. I think the respectful response from the federal team and the facilitators' willingness to step back from our agenda encouraged the tribes that this was a group they could work with. They softened their tone, and the feds responded in kind. And I didn't mention protocols again until the end of the second day, when we were identifying next steps for the group. I suggested that Jon and I draft simple protocols for the group and send them out by e-mail, and if anyone had any problem with any of the items to let us know. Aside from a couple of typos and capitalizations from the federal side, the protocols went unchallenged—and unused for the duration of the process. I am not sure they were even read by the tribal side. (This was a development I wasn't sure I would ever share with my colleagues. To launch into a complex process like this with no discussion and face-to-face agreement about how the group will operate is unheard of.)

There were, of course, challenges as the group began to draft the policy. Tribal members had anxiety about the potential for the Office of the Solicitor to upend any agreement reached. The solicitors at the table assured the group that they were there to support the process and the product, and they promised to immediately flag any aspects of the policy they believed were on shaky legal ground. But the fear persisted through the first two meetings until relationships were forged.

The lack of high-level representation at the table was another ongoing problem. The tribal members pushed their federal counterparts to produce an appropriately important person to join the process. As it became clear that this was not going to happen, they asked for someone of that level to at least make an appearance at a meeting to offer words of support and demonstrate the department's commitment to the process. There was an underlying fear that the policy would end its days gathering dust on a shelf and that tribal leaders would have been exploited in a process that made the department look good for a few months. A higher-level department official could reassure the tribal members to some extent. Their final request was that this elusive person at least address the group by video, or even for a few minutes by speakerphone. This never happened, and I believe it was not for lack of trying on the part of the federal team. The nature of government, the overwhelming press of tasks to be done, the need to respond to an ever-growing list of crises—all of this conspired against their meeting what seemed a simple request.

And, of course, once members plunged into the substance of the policy, there was disagreement about implementation and specific language. Although both sides were often in agreement about the policy's intent, principles, and goals, the challenge lay in crafting language that was implementable. Here the feds had to push back on some issues, even if they believed in the concepts. The establishment of a new position, a Tribal Governance Officer, who would monitor and troubleshoot tribal consultation requests and department follow-through, might be a concept supported by the whole group, but the federal side was forced to be practical. Not only was there no room in the budget for such a position at a necessarily high level, but also there were questions about how that person would fit into the hierarchy. The group agreed to assign those functions to an existing department official, probably in the Office of the Secretary.

There was also concern about accountability. How much could be written into the policy to ensure that implementation would be taken seriously, not only by this administration but also by succeeding ones? Could the DOI-TCT or equivalent body have an ongoing role as a sort of watchdog and evaluator as the department and its bureaus and offices began to put the policy into practice? There were long discussions about reporting requirements that would ensure certain steps were taken in the consultation process and that also would be useful in evaluating the policy's strengths and weaknesses as data were gathered and analyzed over time. This made sense, but the feds were concerned that if the requirements were too burdensome—asking for too much information, too frequently, in confusing or challenging formats—overworked staff likely would not meet those requirements or would do so inadequately. The data would be insufficient and unreliable. The group struggled to find this balance.

The drafting of the policy spanned six months, and by early 2011 the document (agreed to by consensus) had been sent out for tribal comment and then published in the Federal Register for public comment. Even during the comment review periods, the DOI-TCT had a continuing role. Brian Patterson, with Norman Cooeyate and later with Robert Tippeconnie, served as tribal co-chairs and took the lead with federal co-chairs Sequoyah Simermeyer and Jodi Gillette in reviewing the hundreds of comments submitted. The entire TCT met regularly by conference calls and once in person to discuss the comments and negotiate changes to the draft policy with DOI staff. Finally, after laborious clearances through the Office of Management and Budget and the Office of the Solicitor, the DOI's tribal consultation policy was ready for signature.

DOI staffers Jennifer Sisk and Kallie Hanley, who had done the hard work of analyzing comments and revising the document with guidance from the TCT, went into event-planning mode and organized a signing ceremony. We all gathered on December 1, 2011, in the Secretary of the Interior's dark-paneled formal reception room, where Secretary Salazar congratulated the group on its accomplishment and acknowledged the remarkable degree of trust and cooperation that had characterized this federal-tribal effort. He then signed the order adopting the policy, surrounded by relieved and proud committee members. I scanned the room and remembered the anxiety and apprehension on those faces at our first meeting. Now they chatted easily, exchanging warm handshakes, pats on the back, even hugs, as they waited for a photo opportunity with the Secretary and to receive their certificates of appreciation.

"I can put you on the list to see Obama tomorrow, if you can get a later flight." Kallie, with a clipboard in one hand and a glass of punch in the other, interrupted my nostalgia. The Secretary would be hosting the annual White House Tribal Nations Conference the next day, but I had no role and no intention of attending. I thanked her and said that I had just come for the signing and felt well satisfied.

"You should stay. It's going to be exciting, and you deserve it." She lifted her punch glass in my honor. "I'll put you on the list, just in case."

Easily convinced, the next day I found myself in the Department of the Interior's auditorium, seated between two tribal leaders and awaiting remarks from the president. Frank, on my left, was a big Sac and Fox who explained to me that the name is not accurate or proper, that Fox is merely a clan of the Muscouwee, and that at one time a captured Indian had identified himself as Fox and the cavalry, thinking that was the tribe's name, named everyone in the region "Fox." Frank and I chatted about where we were from (Iowa and New Mexico), comparing notes on weather, wildlife, food, and politics. He pointed to the ribbons on his ribbon shirt, red and green, and said that his tribal flag is made up of the same two colors. You can hang it, he said, with green on the top to indicate peace or with red on the top to indicate war. On my other side was a tribal leader dressed in a leather, fringe, and bead outfit, holding in his lap a fur-and-antler headdress. He steadied the headdress with one hand while he periodically checked his iPhone with the other.

And then there was a change in the lighting onstage, and the program began. US Secretary of Education Arne Duncan spoke first, announcing new initiatives to help Indian children succeed in school and new money for college opportunities for Natives. Every pledge was met with applause—on its merits but also because each brought us closer to President Obama's appearance. Following Duncan were speakers, high up in the administration, who summarized the proceedings from the morning's work groups.

The last speaker left the stage, and the lighting changed again. The man next to me put on his antler headdress. I groped for the disposable camera I had bought that morning. A woman in front of me held up her iPad to get a good photo. A disembodied voice announced the president of the United States and Obama strode to the podium, easy, smiling, nodding slightly as he waited for the riotous applause to ebb.

Apparently with no notes or teleprompter, he spoke from the heart about the challenges facing Indian country today. He cited reams of statistics and told stories about people he had met and trips he had taken to visit tribes, and he concluded with as close as a president can come to promising adequate funding and appropriate attention for Indian country in the upcoming session. He mentioned his administration's accomplishments, including the Department of Interior's new tribal consultation policy, signed the day before. As he brought his remarks to a close, thanking everyone for their hard work and attendance, his expression softened, belying a trick up his sleeve. He said that he was honored to have his adoptive parents from the Crow Tribe with him at this event. He explained that he had been visiting Crow country the previous year and that when he was introduced to the father and mother of the tribal chairman, they had formally adopted him, on the spot, as their own son and now a member of the Crow Tribe.

"I imagine," said Obama, "that my Crow parents are grateful that they did not have to put up with my terrible twos or with my rebellious teenage years. They are lucky to have me join their family now that I have a little maturity." Following much laughter, Obama invited his Crow father and mother to the podium. After warm embraces, he moved aside and a little behind them, standing, with his hands folded and his head tilted slightly in bemusement, and looking at them with affection and respect.

He must have admired their quick-wittedness and political savvy, and I could feel ripples of envy through the audience. Leave it to those Crows! They went and adopted Obama first. We could have done that, but now it's too late.

Obama's Crow father made some remarks about how proud he and his wife were of both of their sons, one the chairman of the Crow Tribe and the other the president of the United States. They were also delighted to be going that evening to visit their beautiful daughter-in-law Michelle and their two very special granddaughters Sasha and Malia. He and his wife offered prayers for the gathering in Crow and in English and returned the podium to their adopted son. Obama thanked all the people who had made this gathering of nations possible, including Kallie and Jennifer, I was happy to hear, and expressed his deep appreciation for all those tribal leaders who had come to work in partnership with his administration. Everyone leaped to their feet, applauding. A forest of arms extended in his direction as people tried to get the best angles for their cameras, iPhones, and iPads. I snapped away with my disposable camera, happy to be there in that moment, knowing that I was taking nothing recognizable as the president—as it turned out, not even as a human being. But no matter. It was a wonderful day and a perfect exclamation point to this strange journey.

Since then, the Secretary of the Interior has issued a directive to the department's bureaus and offices to develop a plan by June 2012 for implementing the new policy. At the time of this writing, he is also creating an advisory group of tribal representatives to help him evaluate the policy as it is put into practice. The policy document has not had a moment to gather dust.

The process of creating this new tribal consultation policy for the Department of the Interior was unique in my experience. The fact that this group never needed to refer to a set of agreed-to ground rules in eighteen months of negotiation was remarkable. Most groups drag out the protocols to settle an argument about how to replace an absent member or how to handle a deadlock, for example. My "you'll be sorry" smugness turned to amazement and admiration for both sides of the team. They were reasonable, they were respectful, they understood the challenge the other side was facing, they were patient, and they worked for the best policy possible with great energy and passion. They honored an unarticulated set of protocols based on decent human interaction.

Another lesson for me, and I think for many at the table, was the impact of the tribes' taking the lead and establishing their role in the group. They knew that they needed to seize the drafting job first and put their imprint on it, even if they did not have all the legal and bureaucratic expertise that rested with the feds. By exerting power and setting conditions for their participation at the very beginning, they were making it clear to the federal side that this partnership would be different from other efforts at cooperation, collaboration, and partnering that had regularly taken place with tribes. Well-intentioned as these efforts might be, the feds were always in the driver's seat. And riding along as passengers, even as honored passengers, the tribes could never achieve that equal status that they felt should characterize the government-to-government relationship. This time the tribes were in the driver's seat, and it was an entirely different kind of journey.

Finally, I give credit to the Department of Interior leadership that conceived of, and was committed to, a partnership with tribal leadership that was genuine. True partners listen to each other, strive to understand the other's point of view, find common ground and goals, and move forward together with respect. Both the tribal and the federal members showed real courage and took significant risks to make this process work. Federal members were willing to share authority and let the tribes take the lead. This required flexibility, patience, and a certain amount of restraint on their part. For some it meant going out on a limb with colleagues and management to argue the tribal side. Many on the federal side became strong converts as the process moved forward, excited and even passionate about the experience. Michael Baffrey, the DOI's Assistant to the Secretary in Alaska and a DOI-TCT member, observed, "The bottom line was that the Tribal leaders were the senior leaders in the room. They shared ownership and in fact brought the feds along in their process. I never for a moment doubted the wisdom of the Tribal members . . . the lessons they taught us are incredible."

Tribal members showed courage in the face of risks as well. Even by agreeing to participate on the DOI-TCT, tribal members became targets of critics in Indian country who doubted the sincerity of the process and, like Linda in chapter 9, feared yet another betrayal in the end. It was an additional risk to caucus on that first morning and demand to take the first steps in drafting the policy. The tribes could have chosen to be cautious and wait for the federal side to reveal itself for better or worse. Or they might have let the feds produce a first draft of a tribal consultation policy (a lot of work, by the way) and then responded. Or they might have been reluctant participants, suspicious and holding back, even undermining the process in Indian country to cover themselves in case it went south. But instead, they took seriously the Department of the Interior's pledge to forge a true partnership, and they challenged the federal side to move over and let them drive—at least the first few miles. They risked dissolution of the process on the spot. Or, if the process continued, they risked ongoing animosity from the feds and a very unpleasant negotiating experience. The federal response was gracious, allowing the tribal attitude to soften as the two sides began to work together. Trust was what enabled the group to survive and succeed, and seeds of that trust were sown on that first day.

CHAPTER TWELVE

Conclusion

When my publisher suggested a closing chapter that would summarize lessons learned, I cringed inside. For me it is easier to tell stories and let the truths bubble up, or seep in, or take root, or whatever image suits you. It is a more entertaining way to learn, I protested, and besides, it is hard to distill the work of a career into a few truths. But I know that there are those who appreciate a tidy summation, and so here I go, beginning with two disclaimers.

First, I believe that the most valuable lessons come in the surprising and instructive moments of the "doing"—the stumbling, the gathering yourself together, the persevering, the connecting with others in unexpected ways. The stories in this book recount some of those learning moments for me, and I hope that they have been entertaining and provocative, helping you reflect on your own role in conflict. But in truth, your best learning will come from your own "doing," just as mine has. I encourage you, whether you are a mediator, an aspiring conflict resolver, or simply a curious student of life, to find your own experiences and honor them as the fine professors they are. Look into your past for those times of confusion, anxiety, or revelation when something changed (for better or worse) and reconsider them, maybe in light of this book.

And as you move into your next conflict—big or small, professional or personal—watch for those moments. Listen to those around you in order to understand their motives, their fears, their hopes, and take the same barometric readings on yourself. Watch for moments when taking a risk is worth it, when the potential to connect on a human level might open the door to common ground. Academic education and professional training can give a good foundation, of course, but it is your own stories of your struggles in conflict that will mean the most. They will become part of your own lore, stories you can offer others in the spirit of learning, as well as entertainment.

Second, there is no magic key for resolving conflict. I wish I could reveal my six never-fail steps, my three key elements, my secret strategy for turning a conflict into a win-win outcome for everyone, but in my experience there is no such thing. As we saw in the last chapter, even the most basic rule can be broken with a successful outcome. It all depends on the political, economic, and cultural environment in which you are operating, who the players are (including the mediator), and how they are all feeling on a given day. I am not saying you should throw out the fundamentals and wing it. Setting ground rules, for instance, is an important first step in bringing any group together around a common problem. I always make it first on my agenda, whether in writing or just in my head. But there will be times and places, as we saw when the tribes took the lead in chapter 11, where flexibility will become more important.

What I can offer on the following pages are some guiding principles that are applicable in a wide variety of conflicts—from the lengthy, complex conflicts described in this book to the equally intense personal disputes that many readers will find themselves in. They will, of course, be useful for the professional conflict resolver and for stakeholders in these conflicts, but they will also ring true for anyone who is curious about the roots and dynamics of conflict. We all find ourselves in conflict at one time or another, and I hope the ideas that follow will help you to find that elusive common ground. In the previous chapters we have seen an intractable dispute move suddenly to resolution at the hands of an ordinary person who had an instinct about what was needed and the courage to act. Non-professionals such as Jacob Viarrial (chapter 1) and Thelma (chapter 3), who effected change in powerful ways, are inspirations for us all.

Personality can make or break an agreement. We are not robots. If we were, life would be boring and conflict resolution would happen inside a computer. The unforgettable people in this book were able to shape processes, influence others, build a bridge or create a chasm between warring factions, and either promote or sink a solution.

There are personalities on these pages who brought problems to the process and diminished the group's chance of reaching a solution. Elaine, the environmentalist in chapter 8, was unable to agree to what the others saw as the most benign proposal, that two-stroke engines be labeled to indicate their contribution to dirty air. We can call her rigid, self-righteous, and acting in bad faith, or we can see her as a passionate and heroic defender of her principles. In any case, her particular personality—a combination of her life experience and her inborn qualities—played a powerful role in the group and shaped its product. Neither the mediator nor the others at the table could influence her. Her personality was a force to be reckoned with.

Another example is Jacob Viarrial (chapter 1), whose personality enabled him to take risks and be vulnerable. He invited his critics and traditional adversaries onto his turf to discuss a problem common to them all—the serious contamination of groundwater. Like Elaine and other strong personalities, he was considered a hero by some and a villain by others, and he didn't seem to mind the labels. He saw an opportunity to help his pueblo by allying with neighbors—neighbors who had opposed him in the controversial water rights arena for two decades. He was well aware that his invitation could rile his neighbors more, or that his own tribal members could turn on him for reaching out to the enemy. With a certain arrogance and quirky charisma, he took on what seemed like an impossible task and succeeded.

Finally, the personality of the mediator or facilitator can be a significant factor as well. Consider Ray Daw, my co-facilitator in chapter 9, whose combination of humility and quiet confidence somehow cast a spell of good-natured collaboration over some very contentious individuals who were grappling with a complex funding formula for Indian schools.

Each chapter has remarkable personalities who push and pull, cajole and charm the others at the table, and the outcome is more often than not a direct result of their efforts.

Connecting with others at a human level can reveal the common ground. But first we must somehow set aside the defenses, the fears, and the animosity that are triggered when we are in conflict. These are the emotions that keep us from understanding the other's needs and seeing him or her as a fellow human being. There are plenty of examples of unhappy endings to the search for human connection, wherein the trusting seeker is betrayed or ridiculed or worse. But I have also seen the powerful results when it works. At the risk of sounding naive, I believe it is an ideal, a vision to hold up and strive for as we move not only through conflict but through life.

The story is often the vehicle for making that human connection. In chapter 3, Thelma told her life story, leading up to the moment when she takes that "big chair" as a newly elected county commissioner. She holds nothing back, it seems, as she leads her listeners through one dramatic, painful, startling, or humorous event after another. Polarized before she began telling her story, the group is transformed by her vulnerability and honesty. She has touched former adversaries at a human level. From there, it was an easy step for the group members to see their conflict clearly and the uniqueness of each tribal-county relationship. They saw that blanket solutions—unacceptable to one side or the other—were not the answer and moved toward a solution that worked for everyone.

Thelma's example is from a case in which the two parties had worked together for a year. They knew each other and had well-worn paths to and from their opposing positions. The San Juan County Citizens' Advisory Committee in chapter 5 met for one day only to try to develop recommendations for the county commission that would guide the county in a healthier direction. With the question of a high-level radioactive waste storage facility off the table, the committee members got down to basics. They shared their love of the landscape, their attachment to the region's history, and their commitment to staying put in that corner of Utah. In spite of significant differences—Indian and non-Indian, Mormon and non-Mormon, industry representatives and environmentalists, to name a few—they found a bond that outweighed those differences, at least for the day. They had connected at a human level and were able to produce a work product they were all proud of.

For me, empathy may be the single most important ingredient in the resolution of conflict. If I am able to imagine how that other person feels, to at least some degree, I am moving toward a common humanity between us. And if I can take another step and express that understanding, admitting my limited experience or different background, perhaps the other will take a step toward me. With patience on both sides, we may be able to reach the point where we can share that human bond. Rumi, the thirteenth-century Persian poet, describes that place so well: "Out beyond ideas of wrong doing and right doing there is a field. I will meet you there."

But empathy has enemies—guilt, fear, intimidation—that can undermine our efforts at reaching out to the other. The other's pain may be so great that we automatically put up walls to protect ourselves. Linda, the tribal member on the Indian school regulations negotiating committee (chapter 9), expressed such intense pain from historical trauma that she alienated many at the table, especially the non-Indians. She was courageous, like Thelma, and revealed her deepest feelings with an honesty that was admirable. But many of her fellow committee members could not open up and let her grief in; it was simply too painful. The response from some was resentment that she made them feel guilty and took valuable time away from the process. (An extra dose of resentment was directed at me, the mediator, who they felt allowed her to intimidate the others with her deep emotions.) Finding a common humanity in that situation was more challenging, and the process suffered as a result. Sides remained polarized, and although agreement was reached, most participants felt exhausted and even abused at the end.

Trust is the foundation of a good working relationship. And a good working relationship is the foundation of a satisfying and long-lasting agreement. Early in my career, I confronted the consequences of mistrust. Unwittingly, I drove the man from Mora (chapter 2) into a rage by revealing myself only in professional terms. I didn't understand that he needed to know who I was, really was, in order to know whether we could work together. Especially for communities like his in northern New Mexico, which have seen abuses at the hands of outsiders for generations, someone like me—white, educated, newly arrived—was suspect. To begin to build trust, I needed to listen to what he was saying and try to respond honestly and thoughtfully, without defense or backlash. Once he understood something about me, where I came from and why I was interested in the challenges facing his community, he might consider further discussions and perhaps someday a working relationship. As it turned out, our encounter did not result in further discussion, but it did leave me with a critical lesson: trust comes first.

The Ganados del Valle sheep growers and the environmentalists in chapter 4 were reluctant to come together and skeptical that they would ever be able to trust each other. In a structured, private retreat, the two sides were able to listen and learn about each other's lives, values, and goals and find enough trust to agree to work on a joint project. But, as Colonel Mike DeBow said at his final community meeting at Abiquiu Reservoir (chapter 6), "Trust takes a long time to build, but it can be destroyed in a minute." The fragile trust between the ranchers and the environmentalists in chapter 4 was tested several times during the life of their project. When Ganados del Valle invited the foundation women to hear the community's presentation to the environmentalists (who were also foundation recipients), the fallout was serious. And when Ganados members learned that the Sierra Club Foundation had misused funds designated for a land-based group like theirs, they were seriously disappointed by the lack of support from their environmental allies. At the end of the retreat, the two sides developed a list titled "Future Conditions for Trust," a reminder of the lessons they had learned. At the top of the list was "Expect to make mistakes; acknowledge them, learn from them, try to forgive them." In the final evaluation, some participants said that they had developed a working relationship with some on the other side, and that trust, however fragile, was present.

Roberto Chené, my co-mediator on that project, believes that the biggest challenge in cross-cultural collaboration is to balance two equal priorities: nurturing the relationship and getting the work done. Both, he says, are necessary for a cross-cultural group to move forward, and participants must be careful not to ignore one in favor of the other. In my cases, I often see Anglo group members who are eager to "do something" with the Hispanic or tribal group members. They want to get to work—fix a road or cook a meal or write a plan. They believe that once they are engaged in an activity together, they will have achieved a good working relationship. On the other side, those from a traditional culture may need to have a certain level of trust with those strangers before settling down to work. Like the man from Mora in chapter 2, they may first want to know who these people are, what their values are, how they see the world and their place in it. If either task—the trust or the work—gets ahead of the other, one side will be frustrated. Roberto sees his role as monitoring that balance, helping the group to remember the equal importance of the two priorities. Experience tells me that this dual-task theory is applicable to almost every conflict, with or without a cultural component.

Of course, there are exceptions. The members of the Sandia Pueblo Economic Development Committee (chapter 3) had no interest in establishing trust and building relationships. They were eager to get to work, and I, the misguided mediator, was the one who was desperate to tell all. And in chapter 11, the tribal side of the table surprised their federal team members by cutting short the relationship-building part of the agenda; they insisted on getting down to work on the task before them. They saw the creation of ground rules and other process-related talk a waste of time, although it would have provided an opportunity for learning more about the strangers (federal staff) at the table. To make their point, on the first day they abruptly walked out en masse, returning two hours later to take control of the process. Although they might not have intended their move as a test of trustworthiness, they received an answer in the respectful and flexible response of the federal team. Trust developed, and the partnership moved forward.

Understanding the landscape means more than looking at a map. In natural resource disputes it is obvious that knowing the lay of the land is important, for both the parties in the dispute and the mediator. If the dispute is over grazing on public lands, the location and condition of the land are important, as are the numbers and kinds of wildlife and grazing animals on it. But without understanding the greater landscape, complete with humans, the picture is incomplete, and any outsider will have a difficult time establishing a trust-based working relationship with the locals. Searching for common ground will be frustrating on all sides.

When Colonel Mike DeBow of the US Army Corps of Engineers landed in northern New Mexico (chapter 6), he saw a problem at Abiquiu Reservoir, and in an orderly, hierarchical way he set out to fix it. He looked at the amount of water behind the dam, the existing facilities for recreation, and the number and frequency of recreational visits. He considered his legal authority, relevant laws governing the management of the reservoir, and existing contracts for the delivery of water downstream. In his mind, I'm sure it was a complete picture of the landscape in the context of reservoir management. What the colonel learned during the four public meetings was that without understanding the local culture and history, he was never going to solve his problem, at least not without bloodshed, metaphorically or even actually. He was unusual in his ability to see this reality and to make learning about the area, from those who had been on the land for generations, a top priority.

The result, as we saw, was astounding. He listened intently at the public meetings, and he took in what he heard at a personal level. He empathized with those struggling ranchers, he understood their deep attachment to their land, and he related a bit of his own beginnings on a farm in the Midwest. This was key for the community (previously on the verge of revolution) to join the colonel in finding a solution to his problems.

As the environmentalists in chapter 4 sat down with the Ganados del Valle sheep growers, they soon learned it was critical to know more about the landscape than its biology and forage sustainability. Their ignorance of the cultural and historical landscape sent them to the top of the local grazers' enemy list, much to their consternation. When the community members were able to speak honestly to the environmentalists, and the environmentalists showed that they had listened, things began to change. Most important, though, was the field trip to Los Ojos, where the environmentalists could experience the landscape firsthand and hear community members describe the complex intertwining of the land and its resources, the local economy, the health of the people, and the survival of their culture. With the human piece of the puzzle in place, serious dialogue about a joint project was possible.

Finally, this connection to the land, past, present, and future, means that the land-based communities have the greater stake in the outcome of the conflict. They risk personal loss of livelihood, property, culture, social fabric. A recreationist may be attached to boating on the reservoir; an environmentalist may be passionate about preserving a tiny frog; a land manager may spend his work hours striving to improve the health of a watershed. But their lives are not dependent on whether they succeed or fail. In addition to Los Ojos and Abiquiu, mentioned above, there are other examples of communities with much to lose. The acequia irrigators in Mora, in northern New Mexico, fought against competition for precious water (chapter 2). Residents of Navajo Mountain chapter defended themselves against a radioactive waste facility, which could have changed their lives dramatically (chapter 5). The cattle ranchers of the Malpai Borderlands Group in the Boot Heel of New Mexico saw themselves on the brink of extinction because of a host of outside forces (chapter 7). Communities such as these do not have the option of finding another homeland. As pueblo leader Peter Pino observed to a meeting of attorneys and hydrologists (chapter 2), "We are not going anywhere. You seem to move around a lot. We don't."

Look at the parts, but see the whole. Building on the previous guiding principles, I would like to make a small leap to the following thought. Commerce and government have segregated the natural world into its separate parts, as my friend Jack Loeffler observes in his book *Thinking Like a Watershed: Voices from the West.* Mining companies focus on extraction of minerals, logging companies focus on timber, fisherman focus on fish, and so on. And government agencies have made the same divisions. The US Environmental Protection Agency is divided, by necessity, into a frightening number of offices and bureaus dealing with different aspects of the same environment. The US Forest Service is responsible for forests, and the US Department of Education is responsible for education. And most company chief executive officers and agency heads are not living on traditional homelands where they might be exposed to another way of seeing the world.

But for many traditional people, these elements are inseparable. Those who have lived in one place for generations tend to have a more holistic view of their world. In working with a tribe on a specific resource issue, such as water rights, the conversation may include the health of tribal members, the education of the youth, the survival of cultural practices, the importance of respecting elders, and other seemingly unrelated topics. Those on the other side of the table—maybe bureaucrats and lawyers—are often confused by, and impatient with, these seeming irrelevancies. They want to get back "on track," return to the discussion of water rights. They cannot see the connections.

Making another small leap, I would suggest that failure to see the whole person at the other side of the table is a barrier to resolving conflict. Too often, we see only the part that frightens or angers us. We see labels such as bird-watcher, mining executive, New Yorker. If we are to resolve conflicts and build communities together, we must look beyond stereotypes. And we must be willing to show others the whole person that we are. This kind of mutual learning takes time and courage, both in short supply these days. But we can find examples to inspire us. Committed environmental advocate David Henderson (chapter 4) wanted to learn what was behind the "rancher" label, committed himself to finding out, listened and learned, and was rewarded with lasting friendships.

Power comes in many guises. Conflict is about power, and most often the more powerful side wins and the weaker side loses. Mediation offers another model wherein parties can find their own solution together, one in which ideally all interests share the gains and losses. But in any scenario, power is a significant player. Those in conflict need to be aware of the sources and manifestations of power at the table, and anyone attempting to help resolve the conflict needs to balance power when needed and as possible.

Mainstream power is easy to spot: money, knowledge, academic degrees, language fluency, political connections, and a professional wardrobe, to name a few. In chapter 8, the industry representatives at the table had attorneys, technical experts, reams of research, lobbyists, and travel budgets to devote to the regulatory negotiation process. The environmental organizations at the table could argue eloquently and passionately on behalf of clean air and human health, but they could not muster the scientific weaponry of the small-engine and equipment manufacturers. As mediator, I found it difficult to balance the power. I could not provide resources to the environmental side that would put them on a par with industry. All I could do was try to ensure that there was time for those on the disadvantaged side to learn what they needed to learn, that there were funds to enable them to travel and participate, and that they were treated with patience and respect in the process. Of course, the ultimate power balancer is consensus decision making. With the ability to veto any agreement, the weaker side can be all-powerful in the end, as Elaine demonstrated.

Rural communities, smaller tribes, non-profits, the uneducated, non–English speakers, youth, and the elderly are among those that often find it difficult to compete with mainstream power. Antonio Manzanares in chapter 4 expressed eloquently the inequity he felt. The major environmental organizations were funded to participate and fight for their values and beliefs, while the sheep growers had to spend every waking hour, and probably sleepless nights, trying to hang on to their livelihood and culture. Entering into a negotiation that required miles of driving, loss of income, and neglect of family and community was more than he and his cohorts could handle—financially and emotionally. Although progress was made, in the end the frail trust and lack of concrete support from the environmentalists made the effort not worth it for Ganados del Valle to continue negotiations.

Government power can work for or against you, depending on who you are. The environmentalists in chapter 7 supported the Endangered Species Act and joined forces with the US Fish and Wildlife Service to oppose grazing on public lands. Facing this powerful alliance, the Malpai ranchers suggested collaboration. It was a bold move made in desperation, but it paid off, resulting in the successful and mutually beneficial Malpai Borderlands Group.

The Navajos at the chapter house meeting in remote northern Arizona (chapter 5) were poor in every quantifiable sense of the word. They were unemployed and had limited transportation, little education, poor health care, and very little money, and they spoke no English. Thus their chances of defending themselves against the federal proposal to site a high-level radioactive waste storage facility in the county seemed slim. All I could do was deliver the message to the county commission. (The proposal was in fact defeated, not by the Navajos but by a political move by Utah's governor, another example of government power.)

In chapter 10, law mandated annual informational meetings in a community adjacent to an abandoned uranium mine, now a Superfund site. In this case, four government agencies descended with masses of technical data and stupefying PowerPoint presentations. The irony was that in spite of all the power bestowed on the government, those sent to the meeting were powerless in the face of an angry crowd. They tried to distance themselves from the people they came to talk to, with three-minute time limits on community members' comments, minimal publicity to keep the audience small, limited responses to questions, and no responses to tirades. The tragedy, from our point of view as facilitators, was that reaching out to the community, trying to make that human connection, would have lessened the animosity and created a forum for a more balanced and respectful exchange. This was demonstrated by the US Environmental Protection Agency official who received applause after he expressed empathy and offered to take a small step toward improving communication.

Ethnic power can be very useful, especially in negotiations in which all the power seems to be vested in the other side. Being white is usually an advantage; whites are in the majority of the population and the majority of leadership positions (although probably not for long). In most parts of the country, the values, the norms, the assumptions are those of the majority. But we have seen examples of minority communities whose culture, language, and history are sources of power in a negotiation. They may exercise that power quite consciously and strategically, as did the acequia representatives who opposed the in-stream flow advocates in chapter 2. Or they may be unaware of the impact of what they bring to the table. In chapter 9, Linda's powerful releases of historical trauma and grief had the power to stop progress. It was unclear to me, at least, whether it was strategic or uncontrollable and coming from deep emotion, or perhaps both.

Ethnicity can be particularly effective in contexts in which the dominant-culture representatives are ill at ease or prone to guilt. Switching to a native language, speaking at length on a cultural topic, serving a traditional meal that is intimidating to the mainstream palate—these are among many creative power plays I have seen used to great effect.

What is success? More an art than a science, mediation has struggled to find ways to evaluate its performance. There are so many moving parts—personality, power, culture, politics, and more—that influence the outcome of a process. The method described in chapter 9 identifies three areas in which to measure the participant's satisfaction with the mediation experience: substantive (was the resolution one you can live with?), process (was the process fair and efficient?), and psychological (how did you feel walking out the door?). In that chapter, committee members on both the federal and the tribal sides were satisfied substantively, but some on the federal side questioned the process, and on both sides there were those for whom the experience was emotionally painful, leaving them drained and discouraged. Although the client, the Bureau of Indian Affairs, declared success, I could not celebrate knowing there was profound psychological dissatisfaction for many.

Here is another scheme for looking at the conflict resolution process. Imagine a triangle. On one side is written CHEAP, on the second is written FAST, and on the third, GOOD. Achieving all three is the ideal; the reality, we professional conflict resolvers can tell you, is that if you can get two out of three you're doing well. The processes in chapters 9 and 11 were both relatively speedy and good in the sense that they resulted in full consensus agreements. But they did not come cheap. The Bureau of Indian Affairs hired six facilitators and held five three-day meetings around the West to complete the school regulations. To develop its new tribal consultation policy, the US Department of the Interior supported a committee of over forty people to travel to different meeting sites and committed thousands of departmental staff hours to the administrative, legal, and political demands of finalizing the new policy. On the other hand, Governor Jacob Viarrial's steering committee to clean up the groundwater north of Santa Fe (chapter 1) cost nothing but the price of the lunches, and it resulted in good projects, but it took years and years. You see how it works in reality.

And even if we find these evaluation methods useful, the question remains whether or not the agreement will endure. It may look solid at the time of signing, but as political and fiscal winds change, as staff members shift positions, as unforeseen natural disasters turn our priorities upside down, that celebrated agreement may never be implemented or may be seriously compromised. There are efforts to evaluate mediated settlements years later in order to help the profession learn from its past, but this is difficult for the reasons already mentioned, plus the fact that key players often can't be found. Even determining whether or not an agreement was actually implemented can be challenging. It may have been amended, or part of it may have been implemented, or it may have simply influenced an action or a document that followed without ever having been implemented.

The US Institute for Environmental Conflict Resolution has developed an evaluation tool that it administers at the end of each of its processes. The survey is sent to all participants, agency representatives, and the mediators. The institute is hoping to build a body of evidence that will speak to the value of alternative dispute resolution and help guide agencies and other interested parties in the design of a process, the selection of a mediator, the allocation of funds, and so on. Federal agencies, including the Environmental Protection Agency and the Department of the Interior's Office of Collaborative Action and Dispute Resolution, are making efforts to promote and evaluate the use of alternative dispute resolution as well. These are noble efforts, and the results will spark some lively discussions at future conflict resolution conferences.

These evaluation tools have a common goal: to identify the factors that contribute to successful consensus agreements in multiparty disputes. This is what mediators are taught to strive for. But to be honest, if the goal is a consensus agreement, then I am unsuccessful much of the time. Why am I not depressed about that? Because for me there is another, much more meaningful goal. I want people to leave educated about the issues, with a better understanding of one another, a bit of trust, even, and perhaps an ongoing relationship that will benefit their next encounter. I want to nurture people to be better and happier negotiators, to understand themselves and others in that context. If there is an agreement signed by everyone, so much the better. But if there is some agreement short of that, or a partial agreement, or even absent any significant agreement, I can still leave feeling we have all accomplished something important. It's funny, but I have to stop to think which of my cases "succeeded" and which "failed" in the traditional sense, because for me they are all fascinating, rewarding, and unforgettable.

About the Author

Born and raised in Seattle, Lucy Moore went east to attend Radcliffe College, where she experienced the first of many formative culture shocks. After graduating, she worked for the Boston Welfare Department as a caseworker and later as an assistant to Dr. Robert Coles, author and child psychiatrist. Both jobs taught her to listen to and value the voices of those engaged in struggle and inspired her to strike out and make a difference. She moved to Chinle, Arizona, heart of Navajo country, where her two sons were born. There she taught with Head Start, sold car insurance (as an alternative to the exploitative practices of local dealers), and served as justice of the peace, registering hundreds of voters, holding trials, and acting as coroner. In 1975 she moved to Santa Fe, New Mexico, where she served for a brief time as policy aide for Indian affairs for the governor of New Mexico and worked as a paralegal before joining the fledgling conflict resolution firm Western Network.

Since the late 1980s Lucy has worked as a mediator, facilitator, trainer, and consultant specializing in natural resource and public policy disputes.

She continues to work, as Lucy Moore Associates, Inc., with a diverse group of colleagues on both regional and national cases, often with a multicultural or tribal component. She has a credibility and depth of experience in Indian country rare in conflict resolution practitioners. Lucy regularly mentors those who might otherwise not have access to her field, believing that the future health of the profession depends on its diversity and accessibility.

Lucy lives in Santa Fe with her artist husband, Roberto Gallegos. Her memoir, *Into the Canyon: Seven Years in Navajo Country,* won the 2005 Willa Award for Best Memoir from Women Writing the West. Lucy is a regular contributor to *Back Roads Radio,* a program dedicated to original storytelling.

Index

Aamodt adjudication, 2, 3, 5
Abiquiu Reservoir: history/description, 88–89; uses/conflicts, 88–91
Abiquiu Reservoir/Corps safety needs: advisory council/problems, 96, 99–101; complexity of issues, 100–101; consensus and advisory council, 99–100, 101; control/authority, 89, 90, 101, 102; community meeting, 87–88, 91–92; scoping/open house meetings, 92–98, 102; DeBow's replacement and, 100; interest group factions, 98, 184; land condemnation and, 90, 95–96, 100, 102; needs description, 87–88, 90; NEPA/EIS process and, 88, 89, 90–92, 96, 97–99; resentment towards Corps, 87–88, 89, 91–92, 95–96; results, 101–102; scoping process, 92; structure of Corps and, 92, 93, 94; Western Network changing roles, 101
acequias, 10–12, 48, 88, 91, 105, 187, 190
Acoma Pueblo, 16–17
Adler, Peter, 7
Albert, Dexter: background/description, 148–149; Superfund site meeting and, 148, 149, 150–153, 154, 155, 156, 160
Applegate Partnership and Watershed Council, 115, 116
Audubon Society, 45, 63. *Eee also* Henderson, David

Baffrey, Michael, 176
BIA-funded schools: description/history, 132
BIA-funded schools/regulations negotiations: committee members/facilitators, 133–134; "consensus" meaning, 135–136; FACA and, 132–133; historical trauma, 137–142, 183, 190; process description, 135–136; Ray Daw, 142–145, 181; results, 141; NCLB rules descriptions, 134–135
Bingaman, Jeff, 41, 47–48
Boot Heel region, New Mexico: description/wildlife and ranchers, 104–105. *See also* Malpai Borderlands Group
Bureau of Indian Affairs (BIA), 163, 164, 166. *See also* BIA-funded schools

Carruthers, Garrey, 36–37, 38, 39–41
Chené, Roberto: background/description, 41–42, 184, 185; Ganados del Valle/environmentalists mediation, 41–44, 48–49, 53–54, 56, 64, 67
Chihuahuan Desert bioregion, 104–105
Churro sheep, 34, 35
Clean Air Act/amendments, 125
Clinton, Bill, 163
communities making decisions together, xi, xii. *See also specific stories/cases*
connecting with others: significance overview, 182–183. *See also specific stories/cases*
consensus, 25, 49, 100–101, 121, 122, 123, 125–129, 132, 133, 141, 144, 164, 165, 172, 189, 191, 192; meaning of, 99, 118–119, 135–136, 168, 170
consultation policy. *See* tribal-federal consultation policy mediation
Cooeyate, Norman, 167, 172
Cook, John, 107
county jurisdiction. *See* National Association of Counties (NACo)
courthouse occupation (Tierra Amarilla/1967), 36–37
Coward, Walt, 19–20

Daw, Ray, 142–145, 181
DeBow, Michael: background/description, 87, 90, 92, 93, 96, 98, 100, 148, 154, 159, 181, 184, 185–186. *See also* Abiquiu Reservoir/Corps safety needs
deBuys, William, 115–116
Domenici, Pete, 35, 96
Duncan, Arne, 174

education of Indian students, 132, 174. *See also* BIA-funded schools/regulations negotiations
Edward Sargent Wildlife Management Area, 35
emissions regulations advisory committee (Negotiated Rulemaking Advisory Committee for Small Nonroad Engine Regulations): "consensus" meaning/effects, 118, 121, 123; dissenting member, 120, 122, 125, 126–128, 181, 189; FACA and, 120, 121, 123; group representatives, 118–120; group vs. EPA writing regulations, 119; motivation differences, 123–125; not finding consensus, 126–129; obligations after meetings, 125–126; outside events/politics and, 125; process, 121–123
endangered species: landowners' reactions and, 103, 105, 109; Malpai Borderlands Group and, 103–104, 105, 109, 115; US Fish and Wildlife Service, 103–104, 106, 115, 163. *See also specific species*
engines, two-stroke: description/emissions, 117–118. *See also* emissions regulations advisory committee
EPA. *See* emissions regulations advisory committee; Superfund site/meeting; US Environmental Protection Agency
Española, 1–4, 42, 59, 91, 93, 95, 99
Española and Pojoaque Valleys Water and Wastewater Steering Committee: 4, 135
evaluation tools, 131–132, 190–192

Federal Advisory Committee Act (FACA): Abiquiu Reservoir/Corps, 99; BIA-funded schools/regulations negotiations, 132–133; description/role, 120–121; emissions regulation advisory committee, 120, 121, 123
federal trust responsibility, 162, 163–164
Flores, Amador, 37, 43
Folk-Williams, John, 9, 11–12, 13, 19, 128
Ford Foundation, 19–21, 54, 55, 56
foundation funding: community-based, 20–21; accountability, 9, 12–13, 15
frog, Chiricahua leopard, 103–104, 105, 106, 109

Ganados del Valle: background/sheep-grazing conflict, 33, 34–36, 37–41, 46, 61–62, 189; environmentalists and, 37–38, 40, 41, 47; media and, 37, 40; "sheep-in," 33–34, 36–40, 55
Ganados del Valle/environmentalists mediation: cultural differences overview, 48, 50–53, 186; evaluation, 64–67; Graham suit against Sierra Club Foundation and, 60–63, 64, 65, 66, 67, 184; interviews, 42–46; Los Ojos field trip/problems, 53–56; Pilot Project Working Group members/actions, 58–64; reconvening, 58; retreat location/participants, 47–48; retreat talks, 48–58; ground rules, 47, 49; facilitation team, 41–42. *See also specific individuals/groups*
Ghost Ranch, 90, 95, 98, 99
Gillette, Jodi, 172
Glenn, Warner/Wendy, 105–106
government-to-government relationship, 162, 163–164;
Graham, Ray, 60–64, 65
grass banks, 108, 115–116
Grossman, George, 59, 62
groundwater contamination/Pojoaque Pueblo, 1–5, 191

Hanley, Kallie, 173, 175
Henderson, David: background/

description, 40, 45, 188; sheep/wildlife conflict and, 40, 45–46, 59, 62, 66–67
history of New Mexico (overview), 16–18
holistic view: significance overview, 187–188. *See also specific stories/cases*

in-stream flow legislation, 10–11
irrigators (small irrigators) meeting: description, 9–14; in-stream flow bill, 10–11; lessons learned, 14–16; trust/man from Mora, 12–14, 54, 183–184, 185

Jicarilla Apache Nation, 36
Johnson, Barbara, 116
jurisdiction overlaps. *See* National Association of Counties (NACo)

land connection significance, 14–15, 50–52, 186–187
land grants, 18, 37
landscape understanding: significance overview, 185–186; 14, 16, 35, 149. *See also specific stories/cases*
Leroy, David, 69, 70, 71
Loeffler, Jack, 187
Lucero, Richard, 1, 2, 3, 4

Magoffin, Matt, 103–104, 105, 109
Malpai Borderlands Group: accomplishments summary, 108, 115, 189; conflict and, 116; conservation easements, 108; endangered species and, 103–104, 105, 109, 115; grass banks, 108; Nature Conservancy, The and, 107–109. *See also* Miller, Bill
Manzanares, Antonio: interview/mediation, 42–45, 59, 60, 62, 189; "sheep-in," 33, 34, 35, 36, 38, 39, 40
Manzanares, Molly: description, 43; "sheep-in," 33, 38, 39
Martinez, Palemon, 115–116
Maryboy, Mark, 72, 77
McKibben, Bill, xi, xii
mediation: bias and, 141; cross-cultural group differences/balances and, 184–185; definitions/descriptions, 7; ensuring right people in process, 128–129; facilitation vs., 7; first meeting significance, 165–166; people telling their stories and, 7; success descriptions, 131–132, 190–192
Millan, Cesar, 145
Miller, Beth/Charles, 47
Miller, Bill: conflict with Bob/Katie Scholes, 109–114; description, 105, 109–110; Malpai Borderlands Group and, 106–108, 114
Miller, Carrol, 109, 110, 111, 112–113
Moore, Lucy: Indian country background, 72, 78–79, 136; mediation goal, 192; "naming story," 23–24

National Association of Counties (NACo): background, 24–25; dissolving treaties with tribes and, 25, 29; meeting/telling life stories, 25–30, 136, 180, 182, 183
National Environmental Policy Act (NEPA) description, 88–89; 90, 91, 92, 93
Nature Conservancy, The, 35, 36, 107–109. *See also* Waldman, Bill
Navajo: abuses, 74; tribal government, 72. *See also* nuclear waste storage siting/San Juan County, Utah
Navajo Environmental Protection Commission, 72, 76
Negotiated Rulemaking Advisory Committee for Small Nonroad Engine Regulations, *see* emissions regulations advisory committee
New Mexico Community Foundation (NMCF), 20
New Mexico Department of Game and Fish, 35–36, 39, 44, 91
New Mexico Game and Fish Commission, 35–36
New Mexico history overview, 16–18
No Child Left Behind Act (2001), 132, 134, 142. *See also* BIA-funded schools/regulations negotiations

Norton, Jim, 59, 62
nuclear waste storage siting / San Juan County, Utah: citizens' advisory committee, 81–86; county commissioners / commission, 70, 71, 72, 78, 81, 84, 85, 182, 189; "go to where they are" strategy, 79–80; informing residents, 71–75, 79–81; Navajo chapter house meetings, 72–75; offer / phases, 70; Navajo Environmental Protection Commission and, 72, 75–79

Obama, Barack: adoption by Crow, 174–175; tribal-federal consultation policy and, 163, 164, 165, 169, 173, 174–175
Office of the Nuclear Waste Negotiator, 69
Oñate, Juan de, 16–17
owl, Mexican spotted, 46

Pacheco, Richard, 19
partnerships of ranchers / environmentalists: examples, 115–116. *See also* Malpai Borderlands Group
Patterson, Brian, 168–170, 172
personality importance: examples / overview, 181. *See also specific stories / cases*
Pino, Peter, 15, 187
Pojoaque Pueblo, 1–5, 18, 135, 191
Popé, 17
power: overview / types, 188–190. *See also specific stories / cases*
Protocols / groundrules, 49, 121, 165–166, 167–168, 175–176. *See also* emissions advisory committee, Ganados del Valle / environmentalists mediation, tribal-federal consultation policy mediation

Quivira Coalition, 116

Rael, Arón, 19
Redford, Robert, 35
Rio Chama Valley: description, 88; sheep-raising history, 33–34, 35. *See also* Abiquiu Reservoir / Corps, Ganados del Valle / environmentalists mediation
Romero, Rosemary, 19

Salazar, Gumercindo, 34, 54, 59
Salazar, Ken, 163, 164, 169, 173
Sandia Pueblo Economic Development Committee: facilitating meeting, 30–32, 185; life-story tool and, 31–32, 185
San Juan County, Utah: description, 69–70; population density / diversity, 69–70. *See also* nuclear waste storage siting / San Juan County, Utah
Scholes, Bob / Katie: background, 109, 110, 113–114; conflict with Bill Miller, 109–114
school regulations. *See* BIA-funded schools / regulations negotiations
sheep-raising history (Rio Chama Valley), 33–34, 35
Sierra Club, 44, 59, 64, 67, 125. *See also* Grossman, George
Sierra Club Foundation, 60–63, 65, 184
Simermeyer, Sequoyah, 172
Sisk, Jennifer, 173, 175
Sol y Sombra, Santa Fe, 47
Superfund site / meeting: agencies represented, 154; community liaison and, 150–151; coordination of information / agencies and, 157, 159–160; culture of avoidance, 151; EPA / rules and, 148, 149–150, 154, 160, 190; meeting, 150–160; outreach / refreshments, 149–150, 151, 152, 153, 160; site background / harm, 147–148, 153–154; water deliveries and, 152, 157

Taos Pueblo revolt (1600s), 17
Thinking Like a Watershed: Voices from the West (Loeffler), 187
Tierra Amarilla courthouse occupation (1967), 36–37
Tierra Amarilla Land Grant (1832), 35
Tierra Wools, 34–36, 39, 50, 52,

54. *See also* Ganados del Valle / environmentalists mediation
Tijerina, Reis López, 37
Tippeconnie, Robert, 172
Torres, Luis, 59
Townsend, Jon, 166, 167, 168, 170, 171
tribal-federal consultation policy mediation: background, 161–163, 164–165; Brian Patterson and, 168–170, 172; federal trust responsibility and, 162, 163–164; government-to-government relationship and, 162, 163–164; Ken Salazar and, 163, 164, 169, 173; Obama and, 163, 164, 165, 169, 173, 174–175; plan for implementing, 175; protocols and, 165–166, 167–168, 169, 170–171, 175–176; signing event, 173; tribes taking lead / results, 168–172, 176–177; White House Tribal Nations Conference and, 173–175
trust: significance overview, 183–184. *See also specific stories / cases*

US Army Corps of Engineers, 16, 87, 90, 92,98, 185–186. *See also* Abiquiu Reservoir
US Department of the Interior: agencies involved with Indian country, 163. *See also* tribal-federal consultation policy mediation
US Environmental Protection Agency: emissions-testing location, 118; Sierra Club suit against, 125. *See also* emissions regulations advisory committee; Superfund site / meeting
US Fish and Wildlife Service, 103–104, 106, 115, 163, 189

Valle Grande Grass Bank, 115–116
Varela, Maria: background, 34; "sheep-in" / aftermath, 39–40, 55, 56–57, 59, 62, 67
Viarrial, Jacob, 1–2, 3–5, 181, 191

Waldman, Bill, 54, 56, 59, 60, 62
water resources (New Mexico): *Aamodt* adjudication, 2, 3, 5; groundwater contamination / Pojoaque Pueblo meeting, 1–5, 191; use / distribution history, 3. *See also* Abiquiu Reservoir; in-stream flow; irrigators (small irrigators) meeting
Western Network, 9, 11, 12, 13, 19, 20, 21,30–31, 41–42 54, 70, 92, 98–99, 101, 105, 133, 193. *See also specific individuals.*
White, Courtney, 116
White House Tribal Nations Conference, 173–175
Wilderness Society, 59. *See also* Norton, Jim
William A. Humphries Wildlife Management Area, 33, 36, 55, 61
wolf, Mexican gray, 46

Island Press | Board of Directors